PRISM READING

Teacher's Manual

2

Lida Baker
Carolyn Westbrook

with
Christina Cavage

CAMBRIDGE
UNIVERSITY PRESS

CAMBRIDGE
UNIVERSITY PRESS

University Printing House, Cambridge CB2 8BS, United Kingdom

One Liberty Plaza, 20th Floor, New York, NY 10006, USA

477 Williamstown Road, Port Melbourne, VIC 3207, Australia

314-321, 3rd Floor, Plot 3, Splendor Forum, Jasola District Centre, New Delhi - 110025, India

79 Anson Road, #06–04/06, Singapore 079906

Cambridge University Press is part of the University of Cambridge.

It furthers the University's mission by disseminating knowledge in the pursuit of education, learning and research at the highest international levels of excellence.

www.cambridge.org
Information on this title: www.cambridge.org/9781108455312

First published 2018

20 19 18 17 16 15 14 13 12 11 10 9 8 7 6 5 4 3 2 1

Printed in Malaysia by Vivar Printing

A catalogue record for this publication is available from the British Library

ISBN 978-1-108-45531-2 Prism Reading 2 Teacher's Manual
ISBN 978-1-108-62200-4 Prism Reading 2 Student's Book with Online Workbook

Cambridge University Press has no responsibility for the persistence or accuracy of URLs for external or third-party internet websites referred to in this publication, and does not guarantee that any content on such websites is, or will remain, accurate or appropriate. Information regarding prices, travel timetables, and other factual information given in this work is correct at the time of first printing but Cambridge University Press does not guarantee the accuracy of such information thereafter.

CONTENTS

SCOPE AND SEQUENCE

UNIT	READING PASSAGES	KEY READING SKILLS	ADDITIONAL READING SKILLS	
1 ANIMALS *Academic Disciplines* Ecology / Zoology	1 Endangered Species (article) 2 Losing the Battle for Survival (article)	Reading for main ideas Using a Venn diagram	Understanding key vocabulary Using your knowledge Reading for details Working out meaning Predicting content using visuals Taking notes Summarizing Making inferences Synthesizing	
2 THE ENVIRONMENT *Academic Disciplines* Environmental Science / Natural Science	1 Our Changing Planet (web page) 2 The Causes and Effects of Deforestation (article)	Reading for details Taking notes on causes and effects	Understanding key vocabulary Predicting content using visuals Reading for main ideas Scanning to find information Identifying purpose Previewing Summarizing Making inferences Synthesizing	
3 TRANSPORTATION *Academic Disciplines* Transportation Management / Urban Planning	1 Masdar: the Future of Cities? (case study) 2 A reading about traffic congestion (essay)	Predicting content using visuals	Understanding key vocabulary Reading for main ideas Reading for details Making inferences Taking notes Synthesizing	
4 CUSTOMS AND TRADITIONS *Academic Disciplines* Cultural Studies / Sociology	1 Customs around the World (article) 2 Nontraditional Weddings (online article)	Annotating	Understanding key vocabulary Using your knowledge Taking notes Reading for main ideas Making inferences Previewing Reading for details Synthesizing	

LANGUAGE DEVELOPMENT	WATCH AND LISTEN	SPECIAL FEATURES
Academic verbs Comparative adjectives	Animal Teamwork	Critical Thinking Collaboration
Academic vocabulary Environment collocations	The Role of Water in U.S. Natural Wonders	Critical Thinking Collaboration
Transportation collocations Synonyms for verbs	The Jumbo Jet	Critical Thinking Collaboration
Avoiding generalizations Adverbs of frequency to avoid generalizations Synonyms to avoid generalizations	Halloween by the Numbers	Critical Thinking Collaboration

UNIT	READING PASSAGES	KEY READING SKILLS	ADDITIONAL READING SKILLS	
5 HEALTH AND FITNESS _Academic Disciplines_ Medicine / Nutrition	1 A reading about health and exercise (article) 2 Tackling Obesity (essay)	Making inferences	Understanding key vocabulary Predicting content using visuals Skimming Reading for main ideas Reading for details Using your knowledge Scanning to predict content Taking notes Synthesizing	
6 DISCOVERY AND INVENTION _Academic Disciplines_ Industrial Design / Mechanical Engineering	1 The Magic of Mimicry (article) 2 Technology of the Future (online article)	Scanning to find information Using a T-chart	Understanding key vocabulary Previewing Reading for main ideas Annotating Making inferences Using your knowledge Taking notes Reading for details Synthesizing	
7 FASHION _Academic Disciplines_ Fashion Design / Retail Management	1 Is Fast Fashion Taking Over? (online article) 2 Offshore Textile Production: Why It Must Change (essay)	Distinguishing fact from opinion	Understanding key vocabulary Using your knowledge Reading for main ideas Reading for details Making inferences Skimming Scanning to find information Taking notes Synthesizing	
8 ECONOMICS _Academic Disciplines_ Business / Economics	1 Investing: Two Alternatives to Consider (article) 2 What Has Happened to the American Dream? (online article)	Skimming Understanding line graphs	Understanding key vocabulary Using your knowledge Reading for main ideas Reading for details Making inferences Scanning to find information Annotating Taking notes Synthesizing	

LANGUAGE DEVELOPMENT	WATCH AND LISTEN	SPECIAL FEATURES
Verb and noun forms Health and fitness collocations	Nutrition Labels	Critical Thinking Collaboration
Making predictions with modals and adverbs of certainty Prefixes	China's Man-made River	Critical Thinking Collaboration
Vocabulary for the fashion business	A Life Tailored Around Clothes	Critical Thinking Collaboration
Nouns and adjectives for economics Nouns for economic trends	The Stock Market Crash of 1929	Critical Thinking Collaboration

INTRODUCTION

Prism Reading is a five-level reading series for beginning- to advanced-level students of North American English. Its five levels are designed to equip students with reading skills, strategies, and language needed to be successful both inside and outside of the college classroom.

Prism Reading uses a fresh approach to Critical Thinking based on a full integration of Bloom's taxonomy to help students become well-rounded critical thinkers. Students are guided up Bloom's framework by carefully scaffolded tasks and activities. Following each receptive task, there are critical thinking questions that help students build necessary cognitive skills. Each question is highlighted with the corresponding Bloom's level, or cognitive domain. Each domain corresponds to measurable verbs.

Remember	Understand	Apply	Analyze	Evaluate	Create
name	compare	show	explain	decide	create
describe	discuss	complete	contrast	rate	invent
relate	restate	use	examine	choose	plan
find	predict	classify	identify	recommend	compose
list	translate	illustrate	investigate	justify	construct
write	outline	solve	categorize	assess	design
				prioritize	imagine

Prism Reading focuses on the most relevant and important language for students of academic English based on comprehensive research. Key vocabulary is taken from the General Service List, the Academic Word List, and the Cambridge English Corpus. The grammar selected is also corpus-informed.

Prism Reading goes beyond language and critical thinking skills to teach students how to be successful, engaged college students both inside and outside of the classroom. Collaborative tasks extend the readings and require students to apply newly learned skills in a new, fresh scenario. Students work with their peers on culminating tasks that require them to engage deeper into the content, and their academic community.

Prism Reading combines print and digital solutions for the modern student and program. Online workbooks build 21st-century skills through additional graded language and skills practice in the Cambridge Learning Management System (CLMS). Video and audio resources are available to students and teachers in the same platform. Presentation Plus gives teachers modern tools to enhance their students' learning environment in the classroom.

Prism Reading provides assessment resources for the busy teacher. Photocopiable unit quizzes and answer keys are included in the Teacher's Manual, with downloadable PDF and Word versions available online to registered teachers.

SERIES LEVELS

Level	Description	CEFR Levels
Prism Reading Intro	Beginner	A1
Prism Reading 1	Low Intermediate	A2
Prism Reading 2	Intermediate	B1
Prism Reading 3	High Intermediate	B2
Prism Reading 4	Advanced	C1

PATH TO
BETTER LEARNING

CLEAR LEARNING OBJECTIVES
Every unit begins with clear learning objectives aligned to common syllabi in Academic English Programs.

RICH CONTENT
Themes are current and engage learners. Opening images and discussion questions serve as a springboard for the unit.

SCAFFOLDED INSTRUCTION
Activities and tasks are scaffolded and move learners up Bloom's taxonomy. Students work from the *remember* stage to the *create* stage.

COLLABORATIVE TASKS
Critical thinking is followed up by collaborative tasks and activities. Students are asked to apply new knowledge. Tasks are project-based and require students to work together, research, and present. Tasks are representative of activities students will encounter in an academic program.

CRITICAL THINKING
Receptive activities conclude with critical thinking questions. These questions are organized by Bloom's taxonomy and allow learners to seamlessly move up the domains.

BETTER
LEARNING

EXTENDED LEARNING OPPORTUNITIES
Task-based projects and Cambridge Learning Management System activities offer students an opportunity to learn outside of the classroom. The Cambridge LMS is ideal for the FLIPped classroom or blended instruction.

UNIT OPENER

Each unit opens with a striking two-page photo related to the theme, a Learning Objectives box, and an Activate Your Knowledge activity.

PURPOSE

- To introduce and generate interest in the unit theme with an engaging visual
- To set the learning objectives for the unit
- To make connections between students' background knowledge and the unit topic/theme

TEACHING SUGGESTIONS

PHOTO SPREAD

Lead an open class discussion on the connection between the unit opener photo and theme. Start off with questions like:
- *What is the first thing you notice in the photographs?*
- *What do you think of when you look at the photo?*
- *How is the photo connected to the unit title?*

ACTIVATE YOUR KNOWLEDGE

After students work in pairs to discuss the questions, have volunteers share with the class answers to the questions that generated the most discussion.

You can also use the exercise to practice fluency. Instruct students to answer the questions as quickly as possible without worrying about creating grammatically correct sentences. Keep time and do not allow students more than 15–60 seconds per answer, depending on level and complexity of the question. You can then focus on accuracy when volunteers share their answers with the class.

READING

Each unit includes two reading passages that provide different angles, viewpoints, and/or genres related to the unit theme.

READING 1

Reading 1 includes a reading passage on an academic topic. It provides information on the unit theme, and it gives students exposure to and practice with language and reading skills.

PREPARING TO READ

PURPOSE

- To prepare students to understand the content of the reading
- To introduce, review, and/or practice key pre-reading skills
- To introduce and build key academic and thematic vocabulary for the reading

TEACHING SUGGESTIONS

Encourage students to complete the pre-reading activities in this section in pairs or groups. This will promote a high level of engagement. Once students have completed the activities, check for understanding and offer any clarification.

Encourage or assign your students to keep a vocabulary notebook for new words. This should include new key vocabulary words, parts of speech, definitions (in the students' own words), and contextual sentences. To extend the vocabulary activity in this section, ask students to find synonyms, antonyms, or related terms for the vocabulary items they just practiced. These can then be added to their vocabulary notebooks. Key vocabulary exercises can also be assigned ahead of time so that you can focus on the reading content and skills in class.

If there is a Skills box in this section, draw students' attention to the particular strategy that they should employ during the reading.

If time permits, have students scan Reading 1 for the key vocabulary just practiced in bold and read the sentences with each term. This will provide additional pre-reading scaffolding.

WHILE READING

PURPOSE

- To introduce, review, and/or practice key academic reading skills
- To practice reading comprehension, note-taking, and annotation skills
- To see and understand key vocabulary in a natural academic context
- To provide information and stimulate ideas on an academic topic
- To help students become more efficient readers

TEACHING SUGGESTIONS

Have students work in pairs or small groups to complete the activities. Students should always be prepared to support their answers from the text, so encourage them to annotate the text as they complete the activities. After students complete the activities, have volunteers share their answers with the class, along with support from the text. If necessary, facilitate clarification by referring back to the text yourself. Use guided questions to help with understanding. For example: *Take a moment to review the final sentences of Paragraph 2. What words discuss a problem?*

If there is a Skills box in this section, draw students' attention to the particular strategy that they should employ during the reading.

READING BETWEEN THE LINES

PURPOSE

- To introduce, expand on, and/or practice key reading skills related to students' ability to infer meaning, text type, purpose, audience, etc.
- To introduce, review, and/or practice key critical thinking skills applied to content from the reading passage

TEACHING SUGGESTIONS

Have students complete the activities in pairs or small groups and share their answers with the class. It is particularly important for students to be able to support their answers using the text at this point. Encourage students to work out any partial or wrong answers by asking a series of clear, guided questions like: *You thought the author meant … What about this sentence in the reading? What information does it give us? Does this sentence change your mind about your answer?*"

After checking answers, survey students on what they found most challenging in the section. Then have students read the text again for homework, making additional annotations and notes on the challenging skills and content to be shared at the beginning of the next class or in an online forum.

If there is a Skills box in this section, draw students' attention to the particular strategy that they should employ while making inferences.

CRITICAL THINKING

PURPOSE

- To think critically about the content of the reading
- To give students the opportunity to move up Bloom's Taxonomy while interacting with content from the reading
- To extend content presented in the reading

TEACHING SUGGESTIONS

Have students get into pairs or small groups. Have one student read the question aloud to the group. Have the other student(s) share his or her ideas. Move on to the next question, allowing another student to read the question aloud. Encourage students to ask follow-up questions. If there is time, discuss the questions as a class.

COLLABORATION

PURPOSE

- To build students' skills in group work
- To give students the opportunity to seek out additional resources and apply newly learned skills
- To extend content presented in the reading

TEACHING SUGGESTIONS

Assign pairs or groups as indicated by the collaboration activity. Read through the tasks with the class, breaking down each step. Some steps can be completed in class entirely while others may require students to research, survey, or investigate beyond the classroom. Be sure to plan for multi-day tasks, and set clear due dates for students.

READING 2

Reading 2 is a reading passage on the unit theme from a different angle and often in a different format than Reading 1. It gives students additional exposure to and practice with language, idea development, and reading skills while helping foster synthesizing skills.

PREPARING TO READ

PURPOSE

- To prepare students to understand the content of the reading
- To introduce, review, and/or practice key pre-reading skills
- To introduce and build key academic and thematic vocabulary for the reading

TEACHING SUGGESTIONS

As with Reading 1, encourage students to complete the activities in this section in pairs or small groups to promote a high level of engagement. Circulate among students at this time, taking notes of common areas of difficulty. Once students have completed the activities, check for understanding and offer clarification, paying particular attention to any problem areas you noted.
If there is a Skills box in this section, draw students' attention to the particular strategy that they should employ during the reading.
If you wish to extend the vocabulary activity in this section, elicit other word forms of the key vocabulary. Students can add these word forms to their vocabulary notebooks.

WHILE READING

PURPOSE

- To introduce, review, and/or practice key academic reading skills
- To practice reading comprehension, note-taking, and annotation skills
- To see and understand key vocabulary in a natural academic context
- To provide information and stimulate ideas on an academic topic
- To help students become more efficient readers

TEACHING SUGGESTIONS

As with Reading 1, have students work in pairs or small groups to complete the activities. Encourage them to annotate the reading so that they are prepared to support their answers from the text. Elicit answers and explanations from the class. Remember to facilitate clarification by referring back to the text yourself, using clear, guided questions to help with understanding.
Alternatively, separate the class into multiple groups, and assign a paragraph or section of the reading to each group. (Students should skim the rest of the passage not assigned to them.) Set a time limit for reading. Then do the exercises as a class, with each group responsible for answering and explaining the items that fall within their paragraph or section of the text.
If there is a Skills box in this section, draw students' attention to the particular strategy that they should employ during the reading.

READING BETWEEN THE LINES

PURPOSE

- To introduce, expand on, and/or practice key reading skills related to students' ability to infer meaning, text type, purpose, audience, etc.
- To introduce, review, and/or practice key critical thinking skills applied to content from the reading passage

TEACHING SUGGESTIONS

For Making Inferences activities, have students work in pairs to answer the questions. Instruct pairs to make notes in the margins about the clues from the text they use to answer the questions. Then have pairs meet up with other pairs to compare their clues. Have volunteers share their clues and answers with the class. For other activity types, such as Recognizing Text Type or Distinguishing Fact and Opinion, have students work in pairs and then share their answers with the class as before. Then promote deeper engagement with guided questions like:

- *How is an essay different from a newspaper article?*
- *What are common features of a [text type]?*
- *What words in the sentence tell you that you are reading an opinion and not a fact?*
- *Can you say more about what [x] means?*

If there is a Skills box in this section, draw students' attention to the particular strategy that they should employ while making inferences.

CRITICAL THINKING

PURPOSE

- To think critically about the content of the reading
- To give students the opportunity to move up Bloom's Taxonomy while synthesizing content from Reading 1 and Reading 2
- To extend content presented in the reading

TEACHING SUGGESTIONS

Before students discuss the questions in this section the first time, introduce the key skill of synthesis. Start by defining synthesis (combining and analyzing ideas from multiple sources). Stress its importance in higher education: in college or graduate school, students will be asked to synthesize ideas from a wide range of sources, to think critically about them, to make connections among them, and to add their own ideas. Note: you may need to review this information periodically with your class.

Have students get into pairs or small groups. Have one student read the question aloud to the group. Have the other student(s) share his or her ideas. Move on to the next question, allowing another student to read the question aloud. Encourage students to ask follow-up questions. If there is time, discuss the questions as a class.

COLLABORATION

PURPOSE

- To build students' skills in group work
- To give students the opportunity to seek out additional resources and apply newly learned skills
- To extend content presented in the readings

TEACHING SUGGESTIONS

Assign pairs or groups as indicated by the collaboration activity. Read through the tasks with the class, breaking down each step. Some steps can be completed in class entirely while others may require students to research, survey, or investigate beyond the classroom. Be sure to plan for multi-day tasks, and set clear due dates for students.

LANGUAGE DEVELOPMENT

Each unit includes the introduction and practice of academic language relevant to the unit theme and readings. The focus of this section is on vocabulary and/or grammar.

PURPOSE

- To recycle and expand on vocabulary that appears in Reading 1 or Reading 2
- To focus and expand on grammar that appears in Reading 1 or Reading 2
- To expose students to additional corpus-informed, research-based language appropriate for the unit theme and level

TEACHING SUGGESTIONS

For grammar points, review the Language Box as a class and facilitate answers to any unclear sections. Alternatively, have students review it in pairs and allow time for questions. Then have students work in pairs to complete the accompanying activities. Review students' answers, allowing time for any clarification.

For vocabulary points, have students complete the exercises in pairs. Then, review answers and allow time for any clarification. To extend this activity, have students create sentences using each term and/or make a list of synonyms, antonyms, or related words and phrases for each term. Students should also add relevant language to their vocabulary notebooks.

For homework, have students annotate the readings in the unit, underlining or highlighting any language covered in this section.

WATCH AND LISTEN

Each unit includes a short authentic video from a respected news source that is related to the unit theme, along with exercises for students to do before, while, and after watching. The video can be played in the classroom or watched outside of class by students via the Cambridge LMS.

Note: A glossary defines above-level or specialized words that appear in the video and are essential for students to understand the main ideas so that teachers do not have to spend time pre-teaching or explaining this vocabulary while viewing.

PURPOSE

- To create a varied and dynamic learning experience
- To generate further interest in and discussion of the unit theme
- To develop and practice key skills in prediction, comprehension, and discussion
- To personalize and give opinions on a theme
- To present additional opportunities for critical thinking and collaborative tasks

TEACHING SUGGESTIONS

PREPARING TO WATCH

Have students work in pairs to complete the Activating Your Knowledge exercise. Then have volunteers share their answers. Alternatively, students can complete this section on their own, and then compare answers with their partners.

For a livelier class discussion, look at the visuals from the Predicting Content Using Visuals exercise as a class and answer the questions together.

WHILE WATCHING

Watch the video two to three times in class. In the first viewing, ask students to listen for main ideas. During the second viewing, draw students' attention to key details. After each viewing, facilitate a discussion of students' answers, and clarify any confusion. If time allows, consider a third viewing with the closed captioning turned on. This feature is controlled by teachers and can aid in comprehension. Remind students that they can watch the video again at home or during a computer lab session.

CRITICAL THINKING

PURPOSE
- To think critically about the content of the video
- To give students the opportunity to move up Bloom's Taxonomy while synthesizing content from the unit readings and video
- To extend content presented in the video

TEACHING SUGGESTIONS
Have students get into pairs or small groups. Have one student read the question aloud to the group. Have the other student(s) share his or her ideas. Move on to the next question, allowing another partner to read the question aloud. Encourage students to ask follow-up questions. If there is time, discuss the questions as a class.

COLLABORATION

PURPOSE
- To build students' skills in group work
- To give students the opportunity to seek out additional resources and apply newly learned skills
- To extend content presented in the unit
- To serve as a culminating task for the unit theme

TEACHING SUGGESTIONS
Assign pairs or groups as indicated by the collaboration activity. Read through the tasks with the class, breaking down each step. Some steps can be completed in class entirely while others may require students to research, survey, or investigate beyond the classroom. Be sure to plan for multi-day tasks, and set clear due dates for students.

LESSON PLANNERS

Lesson planners provide guidance to teachers, helping them balance text content with supporting resources and activities in Cambridge's Learning Management System (CLMS) over the course of a term or semester. The following steps apply to each lesson planner, regardless of the program.

At the beginning of the term/semester:
- set up the appropriate *Prism Reading* course;
- send the course ID to your students and/or copy it onto your course syllabus.

Before each new unit:
- open the correct unit in the CLMS;
- assign the tasks/activities to your students.

Before the final class in a unit:
- review the unit assessment and modify as needed.

Intensive: Programs where Reading is 8 hours a week or more, for 8 weeks. You can spend 8 hours on each unit.

Hour	In class	Outside of class
1	Unit Opener Reading 1: Preparing to Read	Reading 1: text
2	Reading 1: review text Reading 1: While Reading Reading 1: Reading Between the Lines	Have students keep a vocabulary notebook – use the CLMS Class Tools: BLOG Review Critical Thinking questions
3	Reading 1: Critical Thinking Reading 1: Collaboration	Reading 1: Collaboration steps that require out-of-class work
4	Reading 2: Preparing to Read Reading 2: text	Add to vocabulary notebook Reading 2: While Reading
5	Reading 2: review While Reading Reading 2: Reading Between the Lines Reading 2: Critical Thinking	CLMS: Reading and Vocabulary
6	Reading 2: Collaboration Language Development	Reading 2: Collaboration steps that require out-of-class work Add to vocabulary notebook CLMS: Language Development
7	Reading 2: Collaboration presentations, if applicable Watch & Listen (through Critical Thinking)	Watch & Listen: Collaboration steps that require out-of-class work
8	Watch & Listen: Collaboration Unit Assessment	

Semi-Intensive: Programs where Reading is 6 hours a week or more, for 10 weeks. You can spend up to 7 hours on each unit.

Hour	In class	Outside of class
1	Unit Opener Reading 1: Preparing to Read	Reading 1: text
2	Reading 1: review text Reading 1: While Reading Reading 1: Reading Between the Lines Reading 1: Critical Thinking	Have students keep a vocabulary notebook – use the CLMS Class Tools: BLOG
3	Reading 1: Collaboration Reading 2: Preparing to Read	Reading 1: Collaboration steps that require out-of-class work Reading 2: text
4	Reading 1: Collaboration presentations, if applicable Reading 2: review text Reading 2: While Reading Reading 2: Reading Between the Lines	Add to vocabulary notebook Reading 2: Critical Thinking CLMS: Reading and Vocabulary
5	Reading 2: review Critical Thinking Reading 2: Collaboration Language Development	Reading 2: Collaboration steps that require out-of-class work Add to vocabulary notebook CLMS: Language Development
6	Reading 2: Collaboration presentations, if applicable Watch & Listen	Watch & Listen: Collaboration steps that require out-of-class work
7	Watch & Listen: Collaboration presentations, if applicable Unit Assessment	

Less Intensive: Programs where Reading is 3 hours a week for 15 weeks. You can spend 6 hours on each unit.

Hour	In class	Outside of class
1	Unit Opener; Reading 1: Preparing to Read Reading 1: text	Reading 1: While Reading Reading 1: Reading Between the Lines Have students keep a vocabulary notebook – use the CLMS Class Tools: BLOG
2	Reading 1: review While Reading Reading 1: review Reading Between the Lines Reading 1: Critical Thinking Reading 1: Collaboration	Reading 1: Collaboration steps that require out-of-class work
3	Reading 2: Preparing to Read Reading 2: text Reading 2: While Reading	Add to vocabulary notebook Reading 2: Reading Between the Lines CLMS: Vocabulary
4	Reading 2: review Reading Between the Lines Reading 2: Critical Thinking Reading 2: Collaboration	Reading 2: Collaboration steps that require out-of-class work CLMS: Reading
5	Language Development Watch & Listen	Add to vocabulary notebook CLMS: Language Development Watch & Listen: Collaboration steps that require out-of-class work
6	Watch & Listen: Collaboration presentations, if applicable Unit Assessment	

INCREASE LEARNER ENGAGEMENT: EXTEND THE CLASSROOM WALLS

How can you increase student engagement? Extend your classroom walls. Creating opportunities for students to engage with course content outside of the classroom not only increases student engagement, but leads to better learning. To engage learners more deeply and to extend your classroom walls, consider flipping your classroom. The FLIPped approach is built on the premise that students can receive instruction outside of the classroom. This instruction often takes place in a digital environment, like Cambridge's Learning Management System (CLMS). Teachers assign students tasks and activities outside of the classroom which tend to be lower on Bloom's Taxonomy. Reading a text and identifying key ideas, or watching an instructional video on a new structure or strategy are examples. Then, in class, students work on higher-order skills, and apply, analyze, evaluate, or create with the new knowledge. Below is a lesson planner you can use as a guide for *Prism Reading* to increase learner engagement by extending classroom walls.

Hour	Before class	In class	Outside of class
	At beginning of term: • set up *Prism Reading* CLMS course • send course ID to students or copy onto syllabus Before each new unit: • open unit and assign tasks in the CLMS		
1		Unit Opener Reading 1: Preparing to Read	Reading 1: text Reading 1: While Reading Reading 1: Reading Between the Lines
2	Students complete Reading 1: text, While Reading, Reading Between the Lines	Reading 1: Critical Thinking Reading 1: Collaboration Reading 2: Preparing to Read	Reading 1: Collaboration steps that require out-of-class work Reading 2: text Reading 2: While Reading Reading 2: Reading Between the Lines CLMS: Vocabulary
3	Students complete Reading 2: text, While Reading, Reading Between the Lines	Reading 1: Collaboration presentations, if applicable Reading 2: Critical Thinking Reading 2: Collaboration	Reading 2: Collaboration steps that require out-of-class work Language Development CLMS: Reading
4	Students complete Language Development	Reading 2: Collaboration presentations, if applicable Language Development: review activities, hands-on activity with language	CLMS: Language Development CLMS: video
5	Students watch video	Watch & Listen	Watch & Listen: Collaboration steps that require out-of-class work
6	Students can collaborate with peers via Discussion Board Review Unit Assessment and modify as needed	Watch & Listen: Collaboration presentations, if applicable Unit Assessment	

STUDENT'S BOOK ANSWER KEY

UNIT 1

ACTIVATE YOUR KNOWLEDGE

page 14

1 *Possible answers*: Many people think it is better to see animals in the wild because they can then be appreciated in their natural habitat. However, seeing animals in a zoo means that people who cannot travel can still see animals from other parts of the world.
2 *Answers will vary.*
3 *Possible answers*: People keep animals in their homes for companionship. Some research has suggested that stroking a cat can reduce stress, dogs can help owners feel more secure when walking or living alone, and pets can help children develop a sense of responsibility.
4 *Possible answers*: Many regions rely on animals for heavy work, such as pulling ploughs or transporting goods or people. Animals can provide materials such as wool, suede, and leather. Animals also provide meat and dairy produce, such as milk and cheese.
5 *Answers will vary.*

READING 1

Exercise 1 page 16

1 endangered 2 species 3 chemicals 4 pollute
5 destroys 6 due to 7 natural 8 protect

Exercise 2 page 17

Possible answers:

endangered species	extinct species
giant panda Chinese alligator Indian elephant white rhinoceros sea turtle	Tyrannosaurus rex woolly mammoth dodo Caspian tiger sabre tooth tiger woolly rhinoceros

Exercise 3 page 20

Added to endangered species column: Arabian oryx, seals, tigers, crocodiles, whales, tuna, sharks

Exercise 4 page 20

a 3 b 1 c 4 d 2

Exercise 5 page 20

1 humans
2 Their habitats are destroyed.
3 for food; for fur to make coats; for skin to make bags, shoes, and sports equipment; for bones and other parts to make medicine, tea, soup, etc.
4 whales, tuna and sharks
5 We can try not to pollute natural areas and refuse to buy products made from animals' body parts.
6 Governments can make it against the law to hunt, fish, or trade in endangered species.
7 They can provide funding for animal sanctuaries and zoos where endangered animals can be bred and then released back into the wild.

Exercise 6 page 21

1 face a financial penalty
2 refusing to buy / purchase
3 against the law
4 provide funding for
5 cooperate by following these steps

Exercise 7 page 21

1 *Possible answers*: perfume, fur coats, leather gloves, plastic bags, some glues, and fabric softeners
2–3 *Answers will vary.*

Exercise 8 page 21

Answers will vary.

READING 2

Exercise 1 page 22

1 common 2 fatal 3 disease 4 cruel 5 major
6 survive 7 native

Exercise 2 page 23

1 squirrels
2–3 *Answers will vary.*

Exercise 3 page 26

1 An invasive species is a plant or animal that arrives in an area where it is not native.
2 Gray squirrels were introduced from North America by people who wanted them as a fashionable addition to their homes.
3 Red and gray squirrels both have long tails, large eyes, small ears, and powerful back legs.
4 Red squirrels are smaller and weaker than gray squirrels. The parapox virus is fatal to red squirrels and they are affected by the loss of their natural woodland habitat.
5 Gray squirrels are larger and stronger, they are more intelligent and adaptable, they can use food provided by humans, and they are immune to the parapox virus.

Exercise 4 page 26
Possible answers:

red squirrels	both	gray squirrels
red in color only 140,000 left not seen as pests smaller and lighter shorter tail store less fat so more likely to die in winter live high up in trees less intelligent can't survive in an urban environment can't eat human food can die from the parapox virus	*live in Great Britain* long tail large eyes small ears powerful back legs can carry the parapox virus	*gray in color* very common seen as pests larger and heavier longer tail store more fat so survive winter more easily spend most of their time on the ground more intelligent can survive in an urban environment can eat human food can't die from the parapox virus

Exercise 5 page 26
1 gray 2 fewer 3 fatter 4 able 5 kills 6 pest
7 few 8 aren't

Exercise 6 page 27
Possible answers:
1 wood products; garden plants, the pet trade, illegal trading
2 because they damage trees, they eat humans' waste food and they carry a virus that kills red squirrels
3 perhaps for nostalgic reasons, because they see them as traditionally "British"
4 because it is an island, and the sea acts as a natural defense against alien species

Exercise 7 page 27
1 *Possible answers:* habitat destruction, disease, climate
2–4 *Answers will vary.*

Exercise 8 page 27
Answers will vary.

LANGUAGE DEVELOPMENT

Exercise 1 page 28
a cooperate b affect c release d survive
e contrast f attach

Exercise 2 page 29
1 weaker than 2 healthier than
3 more successful than 4 more endangered than

WATCH AND LISTEN

Exercise 1 page 30
Answers will vary.

Exercise 2 page 30
Possible answers:
1 to get food
2 They help/protect each other.
3 They both eat fish so live in similar places.

Exercise 3 page 30
a 5 b 1 c 4 d 2 e 3

Exercise 4 page 31
1 T
2 F; The dolphins push the <u>fish</u> ~~egrets~~ onto the shore.
3 F; When the fish are <u>out of</u> ~~in~~ the water, the dolphins start eating.
4 F; The dolphins always use their <u>right</u> ~~left~~ sides to push the fish.
5 DNS

Exercises 5–6 page 31
Answers will vary.

UNIT 2

ACTIVATE YOUR KNOWLEDGE
page 32
Answers will vary.

READING 1

Exercise 1 page 34
a greenhouse gas b cause c atmosphere
d climate e global warming f threaten
g ecosystem h fossil fuels

Exercise 2 page 35
1 It has melted.
2 global warming
3 the Arctic, the Alps, Alaska, and other mountain areas around the world
4 Sea levels will rise, and many coastal areas will be underwater.

Exercise 3 page 38
solution to the problem: 4
changing ecosystems: 2
melting glaciers: 1
causes of climate change: 3

Exercise 4 page 38
1 global temperatures 2 extinction
3 Global sea levels 4 mangrove forests
5 coral reefs 6 farming 7 CO_2 levels

Exercise 5 page 39
1 Argentina
2 Northwest Passage
3 to provide land for growing food
4 asthma
5 methane, carbon dioxide
6 burning fossil fuels and cutting down trees
7 stop burning fossil fuels, start using renewable energy

Exercise 6 page 39
c

Exercise 7 page 39
Possible answers:
1 an increase in land for farming, new transportation routes, increased fresh water, melt water can be used for hydroelectric power
2 the implementation can be expensive, some people say that things like solar panels and wind turbines are ugly, some renewable energies aren't suitable for every country
3 it's too expensive, it's a global problem so one country may not be able to make a change, big businesses can make a bigger impact on global warming than governments

Exercise 8 page 39
Answers will vary.

READING 2

Exercise 1 page 40
1 absorb 2 Farming 3 Logging 4 rainforest
5 construction 6 effects 7 destruction

Exercise 2 page 41
Possible answers:
1 They put oxygen into the atmosphere, provide shade, and are home to many species of animals.
2 to clear land for farming or to provide wood for building
3 The earth's temperature will rise, erosion will cause dust storms and floods, animals will lose their habitats.

Exercise 3 page 44
1 deforestation   2 effects
3 animals   4 crops
5 decade   6 erosion
7 warming   8 habitats
9 protected   10 environment

Exercise 4 page 44
1 ~~olive~~ palm
2 ~~ten years~~ two or three years
3 ~~the U.S.~~ Texas
4 ~~protects~~ destroys
5 ~~oxygen~~ carbon dioxide
6 ~~Small-scale~~ Large-scale

Exercise 5 page 45

CAUSES	EFFECTS
commercial farming by big business	climate change
industrial logging	damage to animal habitats
farming by local people	decrease in biodiversity

Exercise 6 page 45
Possible answers:
1 logging and farming that are done on a large scale by giant corporations
2 The Earth's climate will become much warmer, and thousands of plants and animals will become extinct.
3 Many of the foods we eat and medicines we use come from forests, e.g., mushrooms come from forests and some medicines are made from tree bark.

Exercise 7 page 45
Possible answers:
1 Low-lying islands, cities near coastlines, and places with more rain and storms will have too much water. Places that are normally dry, such as many African countries, will become even drier.
2 As the glaciers and forests disappear, the animals that live there lose their homes/habitats and may die out.

Exercise 8 page 45
Answers will vary.

LANGUAGE DEVELOPMENT

Exercise 1 page 46
1 issue   2 predict
3 consequences   4 trend
5 areas   6 annual
7 challenge   8 contributes to

Exercise 2 page 46
1 c 2 a 3 e 4 g 5 b 6 f 7 d

Exercise 3 page 47
1 power plant   2 greenhouse gases
3 climate change   4 carbon dioxide
5 environmental groups 6 natural resource
7 tropical rainforests

WATCH AND LISTEN

Exercise 1 page 48
1 Possible answers: Aurora, Grand Canyon, Great Barrier Reef, Harbor of Rio de Janeiro, Mount Everest, Paricutin, Victoria Falls
2–3 *Answers will vary.*

Exercise 2 page 48
Possible answers:
1 the U.S.
2 millions of years old
3 the U.S. government

Exercise 3 page 48
a 3 b 4 c 5 d 1 e 2 f 6

Exercise 4 page 49
1 b 2 b 3 c 4 b 5 a

Exercises 5–6 page 49
Answers will vary.

UNIT 3

ACTIVATE YOUR KNOWLEDGE

page 50
1 *Possible answers*: car, bike, motorcycle, rickshaw/
pedicab, truck/van
2–4 *Answers will vary.*

READING 1

Exercise 1 page 52
1 public transportation 2 outskirts 3 rail
4 Traffic congestion 5 destination 6 commuter
7 connect

Exercise 2 page 53
1 The problem is traffic congestion.
2 The vehicle in the top photograph is a kind of
electric car. It could be a solution because it
would cause less pollution and be quieter than
cars are now. It was taken in Masdar City in Abu
Dhabi.
3 *Answers will vary.*

Exercise 3 page 56
Answers will vary.

Exercise 4 page 56
1 a wall around the city and narrow streets
2 Personal Rapid Transit. It is a unique kind of
public transportation that consists of many small
personal vehicles that run on solar energy.
3 an underground rail system, a light rail transit
system, and electric cars
4 The planners decided not to finish building the
PRT system.

Exercise 5 page 56
1 traffic congestion 2 45 minutes 3 solar power
4 not allowed 5 24 billion 6 2025; 50,000

Exercise 6 page 57
Possible answers:
1 An expanding economy means more people
have more money for health, education, travel,
and life in general. A rising population means
there are more people to work and help build
the economy.
2 It will be near the airport, so there may be noise
and air pollution. It might not have good schools,
shopping, or entertainment.
3 It was too expensive, and there were other,
cheaper transportation solutions.

Exercises 7–8 page 57
Answers will vary.

READING 2

Exercise 1 pages 58–59
1 cycle 2 emergency 3 engineering 4 fuel
5 government 6 vehicles 7 practical

Exercise 2 page 59
1 ferry, bus, subway/underground
2 *Answers will vary.*

Exercise 3 page 62
b

Exercise 4 page 62
stress, economic losses, emergency services cannot
get through traffic, and negative effects on the
environment

Exercise 5 page 62
Wording of answers will vary.

advantages	disadvantages
More vehicles can travel at once.	May result in more traffic.
People will think more about using their cars.	Some people may need to give up their jobs.
It has benefits for your health and reduces pollution.	Can be dangerous when traffic is heavy.
It reduces congestion/ traffic in the city center.	Buses may not operate at night.

Exercise 6 page 63
Possible answers:
1 high blood pressure, insomnia, trouble
concentrating
2 People might not re-elect the politicians that
approved the tax.
3 The bus stop might not be close to their home or
work. They might have to wait a long time for the
bus to arrive.

Exercise 7 page 63
1 *Possible answers:* Yes, lots of cities have problems with long commute times, traffic congestion, pollution, etc.
2–3 *Answers will vary.*

Exercise 8 page 63
Answers will vary.

LANGUAGE DEVELOPMENT

Exercise 1 page 64
1 c 2 a 3 d 4 g 5 e 6 f 7 b

Exercise 2 page 64
1 Traffic congestion 2 public transportation
3 bike lane 4 parking restrictions 5 Rush hour
6 carpool 7 road rage

Exercise 3 page 65
1 ~~need~~ require 2 ~~try~~ attempt 3 ~~make~~ produce
4 ~~lower~~ reduce 5 ~~use in an inefficient way~~ waste
6 ~~think about~~ consider 7 ~~stop~~ prevent
8 ~~get~~ convince

WATCH AND LISTEN

Exercise 1 page 66
Answers will vary.

Exercise 2 page 66
Answers will vary.

Exercise 3 pages 66–67
1 flew 2 helped 3 worked 4 had 5 changed

Exercise 4 page 67
1 b 2 c 3 a 4 a

Exercise 5 page 67
Answers will vary.

Exercise 6 page 67
Answers will vary.

UNIT 4

ACTIVATE YOUR KNOWLEDGE

page 68
1 The celebration shown is Chinese New Year.
2–3 *Answers will vary.*

READING 1

Exercise 1 page 70
1 cultures 2 exchange 3 expect 4 greet
5 formal 6 appearance 7 relationship

Exercises 2–3 page 71
Answers will vary.

Exercise 4 page 74
Answers will vary.

Exercise 5 page 74

custom/ behavior	Brazil	Japan	India
greeting	1 kiss 2 shake hands with	3 shake hands 4 bowing	5 oldest 6 women 7 men
gifts	8 home	9 refuse 10 token of appreciation	11 necessary 12 white flowers
business behavior	13 gift	14 both hands 15 read it	16 First 17 no 18 Appoint-ments
dress/ appear-ance	19 well	20 formally	21 formal
punctuality	22 30 minutes late	23 early	24 on time

Exercise 6 page 75
e

Exercise 7 page 75
Possible answers:
1 They might think you are trying to bribe them or "buy" a favor.
2 Brazilians are accustomed to touching, so they might be offended if you move away.
3 Hierarchy is important in Japanese culture.
4 They want to maintain a harmonious relationship.
5 People become offended and relationships could suffer or possibly end.

Exercise 8 page 75
1 *Possible answers:*
Greeting: People shake hands in Brazil and Japan. In Japan people bow, but in Brazil and India they don't.
Gifts: Bring gifts in Brazil and Japan, but not necessary in India.
Dress: Dressing formally or well is necessary in all three cultures.
Punctuality: Arrive late in Brazil, early in Japan, and on time in India.
2–3 *Answers will vary.*

Exercise 9 page 75
Answers will vary.

READING 2

Exercise 1 pages 76–77
1 ceremony 2 couple 3 beliefs 4 engaged
5 theme 6 reception 7 relatives

Exercise 2 page 77
1 The people in the photos are getting married. They are under water, water skiing, in a car at the beach, and dressed as Star Wars characters.
2–3 *Answers will vary.*

Exercise 3 page 80
Answers will vary.

Exercise 4 page 80
theme weddings: 4
adventure weddings: 2
reasons for the popularity of non-traditional weddings: 5
destination weddings: 3
choices for the couple who want a nontraditional wedding: 1

Exercise 5 page 80
a

Exercise 6 page 80
1 ~~suit~~ dress 2 ~~Frank~~ Cathy 3 ~~close to~~ far from
4 ~~theme~~ adventure 5 ~~adventure~~ theme
6 ~~few~~ many

Exercise 7 page 81
1 *Possible answers*: Most American couples choose to have traditional weddings because it's what their family and friends expect them to do.
2 *Possible answers*: <u>Adventure</u>: Some guests might not be able to participate if the activity is difficult or dangerous. It could also be expensive. <u>Theme</u>: Some traditional family members might disapprove. It could be expensive.
3 *Answers will vary.*

Exercises 8–9 page 81
Answers will vary.

LANGUAGE DEVELOPMENT

Exercise 1 page 82
1 We tend to tip the waiter in a restaurant.
2 Formal weddings tend to be less common these days.
3 Anniversaries can be important.
4 Common hand gestures like waving can be misunderstood in a different culture.
5 In Mexico, most old people live with their children.

Exercise 2 page 83
1 In the past, the bride's family usually paid for the wedding.
2 Outdoor weddings are often cheaper than church weddings.

3 Professionals sometimes get upset if you don't use their correct title.
4 Cultural knowledge is frequently helpful in business situations.
5 In Japan, you should always arrive on time for an appointment.

Exercise 3 page 83
1 brief 2 serious 3 separate 4 certain
5 important 6 obvious 7 common

WATCH AND LISTEN

Exercise 1 page 84
Answers will vary.

Exercise 2 page 84
Possible answers:
1 People dress up in costumes and masks and go from door to door asking for candy.
2 costumes

Exercise 3 page 84
1 candy 2 costumes 3 tradition
4 good 5 person

Exercise 4 page 85
1 F; Tens of millions ~~billions~~ of trick-or-treaters celebrate Halloween.
2 F; The most popular ~~expensive~~ variety of candy is chocolate.
3 F; Illinois produces a lot of pumpkins ~~costumes~~.
4 T
5 DNS

Exercise 5 page 85
Possible answers:
1 I think it's more popular with children because they would like to dress in costumes and eat candy.
2 because they want to look frightening / because it's fun
3 In the United States people spend the most money on Christmas. They spend money on presents, food and drink and decorations.

Exercises 6–7 page 85
Answers will vary.

UNIT 5

ACTIVATE YOUR KNOWLEDGE

page 86
1 *Answers will vary.*
2 *Possible answers*: Healthy people eat a balanced diet, exercise regularly, get enough sleep, have a good mental attitude
3 *Possible answers*: They avoid overeating or eating the wrong things. They avoid smoking, drugs, and alcohol.

4 *Possible answers*: walking, jogging, swimming, biking, yoga, tennis, and all kinds of team sports

READING 1

Exercise 1 page 88
a active b reduce c serious d self-esteem
e calories f recognize g moderate

Exercise 2 page 89
a basketball
c housework/cleaning
e gardening
g swimming
b racquetball/squash
d soccer
f jogging/running
h cycling

Exercise 3 page 92
c

Exercise 4 page 92
a 3 b 1 c 5 d X e 2 f 4

Exercise 5 page 92
1 heart disease, type 2 diabetes, stroke, some cancers
2 mood, self-esteem, sleep quality
3 7+ hours
4 a field or court
5 at off-peak times
6 running shoes
7 a park

Exercise 6 page 93
Possible answers:
1 It may improve self-esteem by helping people stay fit, look good, get stronger, and have a sense of achievement
2 People who exercise probably have a longer life expectancy.
3 It's written for adults. The word *adult* appears several times in the text. There are also references in the text to adult activities like having a job.

Exercise 7 page 93
1-2 *Answers will vary.*
3 *Possible answers*: People can become dehydrated or get injured. Some people become addicted to exercise.

Exercises 8 page 93
Answers will vary.

READING 2

Exercise 1 page 94
1 balanced diet 2 junk food 3 Obesity
4 portions 5 campaign 6 nutritional

Exercises 2-3 page 95
1 *Answers will vary.*
2 a 50% b 30% c 5% d 15%

3 laws for packaging, require restaurants to inform customers of calories, tax high-fat/high-sugar foods

Exercise 4 page 98
a 3 b 2 c 3 d 1 e 4 f 5

Exercise 5 page 98
Possible answers:
2 to show more clearly how good or bad for you a particular food product is
3 to make junk food too expensive for people to buy in large quantities
4 to better protect children from the influence of junk food advertising
5 to encourage people to eat five portions of fruit and vegetables per day, to exercise, and to discourage them from eating fats and sugars

Exercise 6 page 98
1 rice, potatoes, pasta 2 milk, cheese
3 meat, fish, eggs, beans 4 candy, cookies
5 pizza, potato chips 6 chocolate, candy

Exercise 7 page 99
Possible answers:
1 The number of obese people has doubled over the last 25 years. Almost 70% of Americans are obese or overweight.
2 *Answers will vary.*
3 If people see that a food contains too much sugar, fat, or salt, they may choose to eat less of it or to not eat it at all.
4 The Malaysian government probably did research on the effects of junk food ads on kids. The research probably showed that the ads had a negative influence on children's food choices.

Exercises 8-9 page 99
Answers will vary.

LANGUAGE DEVELOPMENT

Exercise 1 page 100
We need to see a <u>reduction</u> in the rate of obesity among young people. The first step is <u>recognition</u> that fat is a real problem for young people. One solution is for schools to offer children the opportunity to participate in sports. This would require the involvement and <u>encouragement</u> of parents, who are our main weapon against increasing obesity. Parents can also support the <u>promotion</u> of educational campaigns to teach children about healthy eating.
All of us should be responsible for the <u>protection</u> of our own health, but governments can also help fight the obesity epidemic. For example, they can impose a <u>ban</u> on junk food <u>advertisements</u> that target children.

Exercise 2 page 101

Obesity can reduce <u>life expectancy</u> and lead to <u>serious illness</u> such as <u>heart disease</u> and diabetes. To address this problem, some governments run <u>educational programs</u> and <u>advertising campaigns</u>. These educate people about the dangers of <u>junk food</u> and the importance of a <u>balanced diet</u>. They also show people how to find out about the <u>nutritional value</u> of food. Another important way to tackle obesity is <u>regular exercise</u>, because the more <u>physical activity</u> we have, the better we feel.

Exercise 3 page 101
2 nutritional value 3 educational programs
4 heart disease 5 physical activity
6 advertising campaigns 7 serious illness
8 balanced diet 9 regular exercise
10 junk food

WATCH AND LISTEN

Exercise 1 page 102
Answers will vary.

Exercise 2 page 102
Answers will vary.

Exercise 3 page 102
1 d 2 e 3 a 4 b 5 c

Exercise 4 page 103
Possible answers:
1 two decades ago
2 They will be more realistic/larger.
3 They have already made changes.
4 $2 billion
5 what's in the food we're feeding our families

Exercise 5 page 103
Possible answers:
1 because people might not buy their food/drinks
2 because they want people to eat/drink more
3 a, c

Exercise 6 page 103
1 to give people facts about the ingredients and health value of the food
2–3 *Answers will vary.*

Exercise 7 page 103
Answers will vary.

UNIT 6

ACTIVATE YOUR KNOWLEDGE
page 104
Answers will vary.

READING 1

Exercise 1 page 106
1 harmful 2 helpful 3 prevent 4 pattern
5 unlimited 6 essential 7 illustrate

Exercise 2 page 107
1 *Possible answers*: biology, biography, biomedical, bioengineering
2 *Possible answers*: to copy (mimic), to copy from nature (biomimicry)
3 *Answers will vary.*

Exercise 3 page 110
1 Velcro®, Speedo Fastskin® swimsuit, Eagle Eyes sunglasses, Bionic Car
2 burdock seeds, shark skin, eagle and falcon eyes, boxfish

Exercise 4 page 110
c

Exercise 5 page 110
1 hooks and loops
2 children's clothing, lunch bags, shoes
3 Fastskin® fabric
4 swim faster
5 astronauts'
6 yellow oil
7 strength and low weight
8 the shape of the boxfish

Exercise 6 page 111
Possible answers:
1 It replaces buttons, zippers, and shoelaces, so it's easier for children to get dressed by themselves.
2 It was argued that suits made of Fastskin® gave some swimmers an unfair advantage.
3 Some people might think that it is ugly. Others might find it cute.

Exercises 7–8 page 111
Answers will vary.

READING 2

Exercise 1 page 112
1 power 2 personal 3 electronic
4 Three-dimensional 5 movement
6 breaks down 7 objects 8 Artificial

Exercise 2 page 113
Possible answers:
1 A Slovak company plans to start shipping flying cars in 2020.
2 A 3D printer is a printer attached to a computer than can make solid objects from a digital model by printing many separate layers of the object. It is used in manufacturing to print models, novelty food, low cost artificial limbs, etc.
3 Robots can help people who are missing arms or legs by providing artificial arms and legs that help people to have normal function such as picking things up.

Exercise 3 page 116

flying car	
advantages	**disadvantages**
• 3D freedom of movement	• traffic control • air traffic congestion • mechanical failure
3D printing	
advantages	**disadvantages**
• makes life size models • prints body parts	• more development is necessary to solve some important human problems (implied)
robot suit	
advantages	**disadvantages**
• lifts heavy objects • walks long distances • punches through walls • military uses • helps people with disabilities	• expensive / high cost • short battery life / power • could injure wearer if badly programmed

Exercise 4 page 116
1 T
2 F; Mechanical failure could be a serious problem for flying cars.
3 T
4 DNS
5 F; BMW and Volkswagen are already using 3D printing.
6 DNS
7 T

Exercise 5 page 117
Possible answers:
1 All machines have the potential to break down, and a breakdown in the air might cause injury or death to the passengers or to people below.

2 If everyone has a personal flying car and uses it like people use the roads today, then there will be air congestion.
3 They could help people do heavy or dangerous work.
4 Your arm could break.

Exercises 6–7 page 117
Answers will vary.

LANGUAGE DEVELOPMENT

Exercise 1 page 118
1 will definitely 2 probably won't 3 will probably
4 will probably 5 will definitely 6 definitely won't
7 could possibly

Exercise 2 page 118
1 In years to come
2 before the end of the decade
3 In the near future
4 before too long
5 within the next ten years
6 within two years
7 by 2025

Exercise 3 page 119
Possible answers:

de-	deactivate, defrost, degenerate
dis-	disengage, disobey, disappear
en-	enrage, endanger, enrich
pre-	prepare, predict
re-	reread, rewrite, replay
trans-	transfer, translate, transcribe
un-	uncertain, unbelievable, unfair

Exercise 4 page 119
1 same 2 same 3 opposite 4 same
5 opposite 6 opposite 7 same

Exercise 5 page 119
Answers will vary.

WATCH AND LISTEN

Exercise 1 page 120
Answers will vary.

Exercise 2 page 120
Answers will vary.

Exercise 3 pages 120–121
1 They live in cities in the north.
2 Most people live in the north, but the water is in the south.
3 Each section is built separately.
4 because each section has to be in the perfect position

5 2030

6 It will help millions of people in the north.

Exercise 4 page 121

1 ~~food~~ water 2 ~~lake~~ river / canal 3 ~~570~~ 750

4 ~~12~~ 1200 5 ~~meter higher~~ centimeter lower

6 ~~2020~~ 2030

Exercises 5–6 page 121

Answers will vary.

UNIT 7

ACTIVATE YOUR KNOWLEDGE

page 122

Answers will vary.

READING 1

Exercise 1 page 124

a season b manufacture c volume

d collection e cotton f invest g brand

Exercise 2 page 125

Answers will vary.

Exercise 3 page 125

Possible answers:

1 Inexpensive clothing that is sold briefly in stores and then replaced with other styles.

2 In some shops they change daily or weekly. More expensive brands usually only have a new collection each season.

3 Frequent style changes make shoppers want to buy more. This can have a positive effect on the economy.

Exercise 4 page 128

a 4 b 2 c X d 1 e 3

Exercise 5 page 128

2 ~~High-end fashion~~ Fast fashion designs that are unpopular are withdrawn in less than a month.

3 ~~Traditional~~ Fast fashion is good for the manufacturer because of the greater volume of sales.

4 The biggest problem with fast fashion is ~~theft of ideas~~ the impact of wasted clothes on the environment.

5 Cotton growers need to produce more, so they have to use ~~less~~ more fertilizer.

6 Designer clothing is popular with ~~middle-class~~ wealthy shoppers.

Exercise 6 page 129

1 Ahmet

2 Carmen

3 Sara

4 Fatima; Many people agree with her opinion about protecting the Earth.

5 Jasmine; People dislike her wasteful attitude.

Exercises 7–8 page 129

Answers will vary.

READING 2

Exercise 1 page 130

1 multinational 2 wages 3 conditions

4 textiles 5 outsource 6 offshore 7 import

Exercise 2 page 131

Possible answers:

1 because labor costs are lower and, often, environmental regulations aren't as strict

2 Multinational companies bring jobs to local workers. Workers pay taxes, and this enriches the country.

3 Sometimes working conditions are bad.

Exercise 3 page 131

1 using offshore production to keep costs down in the textile industry

2 The writer is against it. In the thesis statement, the writer says that she thinks outsourcing is harmful.

Exercise 4 page 134

1 Multinational 2 40 3 don't exist or aren't followed

4 117 5 economist

Exercise 5 page 134

Possible answers:

main argument Outsourcing is harmful for 2 reasons
reason 1 Overseas workers receive low wages **evidence:** 1 workers work 14 hours/day, earn < $100 / mo. 2 workers in 15 countries earn only 40% of money they need each month. 3 workers paid by piece, earn only a few cents per item that sells for 100s of $ in U.S., Europe 4 Priya Kapoor quote
reason 2 Working conditions overseas uncomfortable and unsafe **evidence:** 5 Worker protection laws don't exist or aren't followed 6 Workers exposed to chemicals, dust, etc. 7 Noise—author in Bangladesh 2015 8 Buildings unsafe 9 fire in Dhaka
conclusion: Multinationals should share profits and improve social conditions overseas.

Exercise 6 page 135

1 F 2 O 3 F 4 F 5 F 6 O

Exercises 7–8 page 135

Answers will vary.

LANGUAGE DEVELOPMENT

pages 136–137

a supplier b designer label c overseas
d consumer e advertising f competitors
g labor h manufacturing

WATCH AND LISTEN

Exercise 1 page 138
Answers will vary.

Exercise 2 page 138
Possible answers:
1 the fashion industry
2 by hand
3 to work / to a formal occasion

Exercise 3 pages 138–139
a 3 b 6 c 2 d 1 e 5 f 4

Exercise 4 page 139
jacket, pants, shirt, tie

Exercise 5 page 139
Possible answers:
1 Formal clothes. The designer talks about his father wearing formal clothes to mow the lawn and how people now look like they're dressed to mow the lawn for work.
2 No. The designer makes clothes by hand so can't make them in large numbers.
3 He doesn't like the way young people dress because he thinks it's too informal.
4 He wants his clients to try styles that they wouldn't normally wear.

Exercises 6–7 page 139
Answers will vary.

UNIT 8

ACTIVATE YOUR KNOWLEDGE

page 140
Answers will vary.

READING 1

Exercise 1 page 142
a interest rate b return c stocks and shares
d investor e value f recession g investment

Exercise 2 page 143
1 *Possible answers:* stocks, bonds, real estate, gold, jewels, coins, art
2–3 *Answers will vary.*

Exercise 3 page 146
two popular investments, the price of gold over time, classic cars as an investment, the risks of investing

Exercise 4 page 146
Paragraph 1: popular investments
Paragraph 2: the price of gold over time

Paragraph 3: classic cars as an investment
Paragraph 4: the risks of investing

Exercise 5 page 146
1 $283 an ounce
2 It had doubled since 2000.
3 $1800 an ounce in 2012
4 the price will remain about the same
5 $13,000
6 over $1 million
7 $4.1 million

Exercise 6 page 147
Possible answers:
1 the stock market; because historically it has higher returns than gold
2 classic cars
3 Yes; because it costs money to keep them in excellent condition, and because investors have to guess which car is going to become valuable

Exercises 7–8 page 147
Answers will vary.

READING 2

Exercise 1 page 148
a savings b standard of living c factor
d expenditure e income f percentage

Exercise 2 page 149
Answers will vary.

Exercise 3 page 149
1 The standard of living is worse in the United States now than it was twenty years ago.
2 income, number of people in family, housing costs, utilities, food, medical bills, education, etc.

Exercise 4 page 152
Answers will vary.

Exercise 5 page 152
b

Exercise 6 page 152

subject	U.S. Income and Expenditure, 1996–2014
horizontal axis	the years 1996–2014
vertical axis	percentage of income that Americans spent on each category
areas of expenditure	housing and related; food; transportation; pets, toys and entertainment; health
general trend 1996–2012	percentage of income spent was relatively stable
general trend 2013–2014	percentage of income spent went up

Exercise 7 page 153
1 b   2 a   3 b   4 b

Exercise 8 page 153
Possible answers:
1 Because they are nonessential expenditures
2 The rising cost of oil; higher prices for cars; higher prices for public transportation; people living farther from their place of employment, and thus spending more to commute
3 $13,400 (25% of income)

Exercise 9 page 153
1 less; because wages have decreased and expenditure has increased
2 probably not, because the stock market is risky

Exercise 10 page 153
Answers will vary.

LANGUAGE DEVELOPMENT

Exercise 1 page 154
Possible answers:
economy (n) the system by which a country produces and uses goods and money
finance (n) the control of how large amounts of money should be spent
wealth (n) a large amount of money or valuable possessions that someone has
poverty (n) the state of being very poor
value (n) how much money something could be sold for
employment (n) paid work that someone does for a person or company
profession (n) a type of work that needs special training or education
expense (n) the money that you spend on something economic
economic (adj) relating to the system by which a country produces and uses goods and money
financial (adj) relating to money or how money is managed
wealthy (adj) having lots of money and possessions; rich
poor (adj) having very little money or few possessions
valuable (adj) valuable objects could be sold for a lot of money
employed (adj) working for a company that pays you a wage
professional (adj) relating to a job that needs special training or education
expensive (adj) costing a lot of money

Exercise 2 page 154
1 economy   2 financial   3 wealthy   4 poverty
5 valuable   6 employment   7 Professional
8 expensive

Exercise 3 page 155
1 market   2 purchase   3 consumers   4 trend
5 demand   6 Revenue   7 supply

WATCH AND LISTEN

Exercise 1 page 156
Possible answers:
1 New York City, London, Tokyo, Frankfurt, Shanghai, Singapore
2 People lose their jobs. / People don't have money.
3 *Answers will vary.*

Exercise 2 page 156
Answers will vary.

Exercise 3 page 156
1 New York
2 October 29, 1929
3 It was the beginning of the Great Depression, where stock prices fell.
4 banks, companies, people who lost their jobs.

Exercise 4 page 157
1 c   2 e   3 d   4 a   5 b

Exercise 5 page 157
Possible answers:
1 October 29, 1929
2 millions of people
3 They fell 90%.
4 on Wall Street in New York City
5 computers and electronic boards

Exercise 6 page 157
Possible answers:
1 yes
2 Because the economies of countries are connected. The US lent money to Europe after World War I. When the US economy collapsed, money stopped being sent to Europe, and economies in European countries collapsed as well, resulting in job losses.
3 Computers let people get information quickly. More people can get stock information with computers.

Exercises 7–8 page 157
Answers will vary.

VIDEO SCRIPTS

UNIT 1

▶ **Great Egret and Dolphin Fishing Teamwork**

The marshes of South Carolina are the location of an interesting fish tale.

There, these dolphins and egrets work together in a very special way.

These egrets are experts on the dolphins' behavior.

The moment a dolphin comes to the surface of the water and checks the nearest mud bank, the birds get ready for action.

Then, it happens. The dolphins push the fish onto the shore.

When the fish are out of the water, the dolphins start eating. But the egrets also join them for dinner.

This is the only place in the world where you can see this kind of behavior.

Strangely, the dolphins always use their right sides to push the fish to the shore.

The young dolphins learn this fishing technique from their parents, and so do the young egrets. Many of the birds now depend on the dolphins for their food. They never even fish for themselves.

These egrets and dolphins demonstrate the ability of different animal species to work together in order to survive.

UNIT 2

▶ **Colorado River, Grand Canyon, Yosemite**

Some of the world's most beautiful natural environments are in the southwestern United States.

In just a few million years, the Colorado River has cut through parts of Arizona to form the Grand Canyon.

The Grand Canyon is 277 miles long and, in some places, 18 miles wide. At its deepest places, the river is a mile below the top of the canyon. It shows the effects of water and weather on the Earth's surface.

Its oldest rocks are almost 2 billion years old, nearly half the age of the Earth. This is the world's largest canyon, and the weather here can change dramatically. In the same day you can have hot, dry weather, followed by wind and snow. And every year the Colorado River

cuts a little deeper into the bottom of the Grand Canyon.

Water also formed Carlsbad Caverns in New Mexico. Carlsbad is the largest, deepest cave system in North America. Even today water continues to change the inside of the caves.

The results are spectacular.

Finally, high in the Sierra Mountains of California is Yosemite National Park. Its famous landmark Half Dome was made by the frozen water in a glacier moving through the canyon.

Today the glaciers are gone, but water from the melting mountain snow flows throughout the national park.

Yosemite Falls drops nearly 2,500 feet—it's the tallest waterfall in North America.

UNIT 3

▶ **The Jumbo Jet**

Narrator: In 1969, a true giant of the skies first took flight. It could cross the Atlantic with enough fuel and twice as many passengers as any airplane before it. Now, there are nearly 1,000 of them. Each one is able to fly over 14 hours to their destinations without stopping. It's the 747—the jumbo jet—and this is the very first one. Jimmy Barber helped build this very plane.

Jimmy Barber: Eight months straight you worked on the airplane, and we didn't just work, err, eight hours a day. Sometimes we worked 12 or more hours a day. And if it was necessary to sleep in your car in a parking lot, that's what you did. It was a highlight in my whole life was this aircraft, you know. Yeah. Wow, this is great.

Narrator: This is the first time Jimmy has been aboard since he worked on it over 45 years ago.

Jimmy Barber: This is great.

Narrator: When it first flew, this was the most modern plane in the air. It was the first double-decker jet in history with a fancy first-class lounge upstairs.

Jimmy Barber: And the upper deck, one airline turned that into a disco and put a dance floor up there. Another airline put piano bars in his … in these airplanes.

Narrator: But it was the enormous space downstairs that changed commercial air travel forever. With room for around 500 people, it started the age of low-cost air travel.

Since its first flight, engineers have redesigned the 747 fifteen times. Today it flies further and faster than ever before

UNIT 4

▶ Halloween by the Numbers

Now, a little Halloween by the numbers. Tens of millions of trick-or-treaters are expected to hit the streets tomorrow. We purchase an estimated 600 million pounds of candy for Halloween, and if you haven't gotten to it yet, we are told that the most popular variety is—no surprise—chocolate. Other top costume choices include witches, pirates, and Batman. More than a billion pounds of pumpkins were grown last year. Illinois is the nation's number one pumpkin producing state. As for the origin of trick-or-treating, it is thought to have evolved from a Celtic tradition of putting out treats to placate the spirits who roam the streets during a sacred festival that marked the end of the Celtic year. Finally, you may be surprised to learn that there is nothing frightening about Halloween if you are a retailer. It is the second highest grossing holiday after Christmas. The National Retail Federation estimates the average person will spend nearly $75 on decorations, costumes and, of course, candy.

UNIT 5

▶ Nutrition Labels

Reporter: Today the Food and Drug Administration proposed a food label makeover. Jeff Pegues tells us it includes a reality check that some feel is long overdue.

Jeff Pegues: What and how people eat have changed. Now, for the first time in two decades, the labels on foods will change, too. The calories will be featured more prominently, and any added sugars or sweeteners will be listed as well. FDA commissioner Margaret Hamburg.

Margaret Hamburg: We're also asking for a change in serving size to reflect the realities of what people are eating.

Jeff Pegues: Here's what that means. The label on this pint of Ben & Jerry's chocolate chip cookie dough ice cream says each halfcup serving has 280 calories and 25% of the fat we should eat every day. Under the FDA proposal, the serving size would be a more realistic cup, which means each serving would contain 560 calories and 50% fat. At least publically, the food and beverage industry has been supportive. The Grocery Manufacturers Association says it's critical that any changes ultimately serve to inform and not confuse consumers. Some beverage companies, like PepsiCo, have already made changes, but what may be difficult for the industry to swallow, the overall price tag. A senior Obama administration official says the cost of implementing the changes could reach 2 billion dollars. First Lady Michelle Obama is a driving force behind the new labels.

Michelle Obama: As consumers and as parents, we have a right to understand what's in the food we're feeding our families, because that's really the only way that we can make informed choices.

Reporter: This is just a proposal, so there will be a public comment period. Nora, the FDA says it may be two years before consumers see these new labels on food in stores.

UNIT 6

▶ China's Man-made River

History is filled with stories of humans overcoming obstacles through discovery and invention. Take an enormous country like China. What do you do when most of your people live in the north, in cities like Beijing, but most of your water is in the south? You build an artificial river to bring water from the south to the north.

This river will be about 750 miles long when it is finished in 2030.

And this is it. A giant raised canal, or aqueduct—one of the largest engineering projects in the world.

Chinese workers and engineers are building the river piece by piece, in separate sections.

Each section starts as a metal framework.

A team of 20 people build the metal frame.

Then the concrete is added.

Finally, the section is moved into place using one of the world's most powerful cranes.

Each section weighs 1,200 tons—more than three commercial airplanes.

This woman operates the crane. It's a very important job, and it takes great skill.

She must work very carefully so that each section of the artificial river is in the perfect position.

The water will flow north to Beijing without using any pumps.

So the end of each section must be exactly 1 centimeter lower than the other end.

When the river is finished and operating in 2030, the water from the south will reach millions of Chinese people in the north.

UNIT 7

▶ **A Life Tailored Around Clothes**

Edgar Pomeroy: I'm Edgar Pomeroy. I grew up in Savannah, Georgia, and I knew I wanted to be a fashion designer when I was ten years old. Well, every day I used to watch my father get dressed because I would be watching cartoons or something on TV in their bedroom. And he was always putting on pinstripe suits and polka-dot ties and waistcoats and dressed to the nines, as they say. He was the only one I've ever known to mow the lawn in a Brooks Brothers button-down and khaki pants, and Weejuns, might I add. That's really how it all began.

Father: But you've always been able to put fabrics and colors together.

Edgar Pomeroy: Yeah, but look who I'm talking to. We're bespoke tailors as well as I'm more of a designer so we make our shirts and suits and all our clothes right here. We don't source anything out.

This is for a client that I'm seeing tomorrow. All the stripes match. The plaids come down. This is detail.

I'm upstairs when I'm in town pretty much all the time, checking the jackets and pants and seeing who's doing what. It has to fit. You can do the most beautiful cloth in the world but if you botch the cutting, it's over.

It's just another piece of cloth that should be burned up in the floor. It got very lackadaisical in the 90s when the dot-com era came into play. And I was kind of disappointed because people kind of started dressing way down.

Some even looked like they just mowed their lawn. I dress people who love clothes. People who want to stand out, elegantly, of course. But they're dandies.

I didn't want to overkill this because you're conservative.

I go to their houses in Chicago, I go to L.A., I go to Baltimore, New York, London. I go all over. You know, I build a trust with them and I design for them. What I do is get to know their personality. If I go to their office or home, I look around, I see how it's decorated, I look at pictures, and I design around their personality. But I want them to take a little bit of a step out of their comfort zone. A little one, just to try. I let the client have the stage. I just kind of help them get to the stage.

UNIT 8

▶ **Stock Market Crash of 1929**

Narrator: On October 29, 1929, the New York Stock Exchange had its worst day ever—Black Tuesday. The stock market crashed, and investors lost billions of dollars in a single day. That day was the end of a decade of a strong U.S economy. It was the beginning of the Great Depression, the worst economic period in modern world history. During the next two years, stock prices fell 90%, banks and companies failed, and millions of people around the world lost their jobs.

Today you can visit the Museum of Financial History on Wall Street, in New York City, to learn more about what happened.

Man: So what we have here is the physical tape from October 29th, that Black Tuesday, and it's quite an important piece, it tells a great story.

Narrator: This is a replica of the machine that produced that ticker tape. The name *ticker tape* comes from the sound of the machine as it printed out the price of stocks and shares. But since the early 1970s, computers and electronic boards have reported the ups and downs in the stock market.

Name: _____ Date: _____

Read the article. Then answer the questions that follow.

1 The Portuguese man-of-war got its name because it looks like a war ship on the water's surface. It is also as dangerous as one. Some people think it is a jellyfish, but this sea creature is actually a group of tiny animals working together. The Portuguese man-of-war prefers warm waters such as the tropical parts of the oceans, which are good sources of food. They float in groups, sometimes with more than 1,000 men-of-war. They cannot swim on their own, so they float wherever the wind or the sea takes them.

2 Although the man-of-war floats on the surface, its tentacles are under the water. The tentacles are the long, thin parts of its body that it uses to get food. The tentacles help the man-of-war **survive**. They can be up to 165 feet (50 meters) long. Each of these tentacles has poison, which the man-of-war uses to kill fish and other small sea creatures that swim into its tentacles. In fact, even when it is dead, this creature can still sting. Whereas the sting is **fatal** for most fish, it rarely is for humans, but it is extremely painful.

3 **Common** signs that you have been stung are a feeling of burning and a redness of the skin. If you are stung, you should take the following steps. First, remove any parts of the tentacles that may be stuck to your skin. Be careful not to touch them with your fingers. Then, apply salt water or fresh water. You can also apply heat or cold to help the pain. People who have more serious reactions should see a doctor.

PART A: KEY SKILLS

1 READING FOR MAIN IDEAS Circle the best title for the text.

a Signs You've Been Stung   b Tropical Fish   c A Dangerous Sea Creature

2 Write the paragraph number next to the main ideas.

a The tentacles of the Portuguese man-of-war _____

b A general description of the Portuguese man-of-war _____

c The sting of the Portuguese man-of-war _____

PART B: ADDITIONAL SKILLS

3 Write *T* (true) or *F* (false) next to the statements. Correct the false statements.

_____ 1 The Portuguese man-of-war is not a jellyfish.

_____

_____ 2 The Portuguese man-of-war swims in warm waters.

_____

_____ 3 The tentacles can grow up to 50 feet long.

_____

_____ 4 The sting is often fatal to humans.

_____

_____ 5 A dead Portuguese man-of-war is still dangerous.

_____

_____ 6 Fresh or salt water is a good way to help the pain of a Portuguese man-of-war's sting.

_____

Name: _____ Date: _____

PART A: KEY VOCABULARY

1 Choose the correct word to complete each sentence.

1 The burning of fossil fuels is a _____ cause of air pollution. It caused 70% of all air pollution in the U.S. in 2014.

   a fatal   b major

2 It is important to use clean energy that does not _____ the air.

   a pollute   b protect

3 _____ used in farming and cleaning are harmful when they get into the air.

   a Species   b Chemicals

4 Air pollution can cause lung _____ , which makes it difficult for a person to breathe.

   a disease   b chemical

5 Smoking can be _____ . It leads to more than 480,000 deaths per year in the U.S.

   a common   b fatal

6 _____ increases in air pollution, more and more people in the town are becoming sick.

   a Major   b Due to

7 Other causes of air pollution, such as smoke from forest fires and volcanoes, are _____ .

   a native   b natural

8 Humans are not the only ones who suffer from air pollution. Animal and plant _____ are affected too.

   a species   b diseases

9 A _____ sign of a sick plant is yellow leaves. You can often see this in cities and in forests.

   a common   b cruel

2 Complete the paragraph with the correct form of the words in the box.

| cruel   destroy   endangered   native   protect   survive |

Animals that are (1) _____ are disappearing from our world. Why are they dying? Why can they not (2) _____ ? In some cases, people (3) _____ their habitats by cutting down trees to use the land. Then the animals have nowhere to live. In these cases, the plants that are (4) _____ to the habitat are also affected. They can no longer grow. This means that if we can (5) _____ a habitat, we can help both the plants and animals there. It is (6) _____ to think that the world is just for humans. We need to share the earth with plants and animals, and not hurt them.

PART B: LANGUAGE DEVELOPMENT

3 ACADEMIC VERBS Choose the correct verb to complete each sentence.

1 Some animals use chemicals to communicate. They _____ a chemical when there is danger to let other animals know.

   a release   **b** contrast

2 Many animals _____ to survive. They work in groups to hunt or protect themselves from other animals.

   a cooperate   **b** attach

3 Some seeds _____ themselves to animal fur or bird feathers. Then they are carried to other places and grow there.

   a release   **b** attach

4 Air pollution _____ our water. The pollution mixes with rain and gets into rivers, lakes, and oceans.

   a cooperates   **b** affects

5 In my presentation, I will compare and _____ animals that work together to hunt and animals that hunt alone.

   a cooperate   **b** contrast

4 COMPARATIVE ADJECTIVES Complete the sentences using the comparative form.

1 *Whale sharks do not have sharp teeth or a powerful bite, unlike tiger sharks.*

   A tiger shark's bite is _____ (strong) a whale shark's.

2 *The tiger shark is not at risk of extinction, whereas the whale shark is endangered.*

   The tiger shark is _____ (common) the whale shark.

3 *Whale sharks do not attack humans, whereas tiger sharks have attacked 111 humans since records began.*

   Tiger sharks are _____ (dangerous) whale sharks.

4 *The red squirrel has a typical head-and-body length of 7.5 to 9 inches, whereas the gray squirrel has a typical head-and-body length of 9 and 12 inches.*

   The gray squirrel is _____ (large) the red squirrel.

5 *Gray squirrels weigh more than red squirrels.*

   Gray squirrels are _____ (heavy) red squirrels.

Prism Reading 2 © Cambridge University Press 2018 **Photocopiable**

Name: _____ Date: _____

Read the article. Then answer the questions that follow.

The Consequences of Climate Change on Glaciers

1 Glaciers are important to our world. They cover about 10% of earth and hold 75% of the world's fresh water. These huge moving masses of ice start as snow, turn to ice, and eventually crash into the sea.

2 Across the globe glaciers are melting, leading to an increase in water and a rise in sea levels. Melting mountain glaciers are responsible for one-third of the increase in sea levels. Twenty-five percent of that increase is from Alaska's mountain glaciers, which are melting because of climate change. In fact, for the past 19 years, 75 billion tons of water pour into the sea from the melting glaciers in Alaska every year.

3 To better understand the impact of climate change on Alaska's glaciers, scientists have followed the streams that run through these slowly disappearing mountains of ice. These fast rivers of freezing water are formed as glaciers melt and are an important measure of the health of a glacier. Every glacier is in a careful balance. The amount of snow falling in winter must equal the amount that melts in the summer. If that balance changes, and there is less snow than the amount that melts in the summer, the glacier will begin to disappear. Right now, that is what is happening. These glaciers are melting faster than they are growing, and when a glacier disappears, it is gone for good.

4 As the glaciers melt, the rise in sea level threatens our world's ecosystems. Already, many of the world's islands are in danger of flooding. In addition, fish and other sea life depend on water temperatures which are also changing. The effects of global warming threaten human and animal life. We cannot predict the future, but we know the consequences of climate change are serious.

PART A: KEY SKILLS

1 READING FOR DETAILS Read the article again and complete the chart with supporting details.

Definition of glaciers	a
Percentage of the world's fresh water in glaciers	b
Percentage of increase in sea level from Alaska's melting glaciers	c
Reason glaciers disappear	d
Example of the effects of climate change on an ecosystem	e

PART B: ADDITIONAL SKILLS

2 Complete the sentences with the correct form of the words or numbers in the box.

> grow   ice   melt   rise   snow   1/3   19   25   75

1 When temperatures increase, glaciers _____ .
2 If glaciers continue to melt, the sea level will continue to _____ .
3 Glaciers begin as snow and then turn into _____ .
4 The amount of _____ in winter must equal the amount that melts in summer for glaciers to be healthy.
5 Alaskan glaciers are melting faster than they are _____ .
6 The percentage of the melting mountain glaciers that Alaska is responsible for is _____ %.
7 Water from melting mountain glaciers account for _____ of the increase in the sea levels.
8 Glaciers hold _____ % of the world's fresh water.
9 Every year 75 _____ tons of water melt into the sea from glaciers in Alaska.
10 The amount of water from melting glaciers in Alaska has been the same every year for _____ years.

Name: _____ Date: _____

PART A: KEY VOCABULARY

1 Complete the paragraph with the correct form of the words in the box.

| atmosphere | greenhouse gas | global warming | logging | rainforest | threaten |

(1) _____ destroys land, and the consequences of cutting down trees are serious. First, this often happens in the (2) _____ , which have some of the world's most diverse species of plants growing in this wet climate. The plants and animals that live in this area are (3) _____ as their homes are destroyed. In addition, this practice contributes to the problem of (4) _____ and rising temperatures. Because the trees are no longer there to absorb carbon dioxide, it goes into the (5) _____ , and is added to other (6) _____ , like methane.

2 Match the sentence halves.

1 The **destruction** of forests leads to _____   a carbon dioxide and give off oxygen.

2 The **climate** is _____   b breathing problems.

3 An **ecosystem** is _____   c oil, which is found in the earth.

4 One **effect** of air pollution on people is _____   d increasing temperatures.

5 The **cause** of melting glaciers is _____   e more flooding due to fewer trees.

6 **Farming** is _____   f the weather in an area over a long period of time.

7 An example of a **fossil fuel** is _____   g the use of land to grow food and raise animals.

8 Trees **absorb** _____   h the process of building houses, schools, and other structures.

9 **Construction** is _____   i the plants and animals in an area and their effect on each other and the environment.

PART B: LANGUAGE DEVELOPMENT

3 ACADEMIC VOCABULARY Complete the sentences with the correct form of the word or phrase from the box.

annual   challenge   contribute to   predict   trend

1 Many of the environmental _____ we face are problems that humans created.

2 Weather reporters _____ temperatures and weather patterns using advanced equipment.

3 The _____ rainfall in California has fallen for the past five years.

4 One _____ we can see in the last ten years is more people sharing cars and riding together.

5 Many human behaviors, like burning fossil fuels, _____ climate change.

4 ENVIRONMENT COLLOCATIONS Complete the sentences with the correct form of the words in the box.

climate   environmental   greenhouse   plant   tropical

1 Power _____ often burn fossil fuels to produce electricity.

2 Many _____ groups, like the Sierra Club and Audubon Society, raise money to protect plants and animals.

3 Most scientists agree that human activity is a major cause of today's _____ change.

4 The largest _____ rainforest is the Amazon Basin in South America.

5 The increase in _____ gases in the atmosphere is one of the main causes of global warming.

Name: _____   Date: _____

PART A: KEY SKILLS

1 PREDICTING CONTENT USING VISUALS Look at the photos in the reading, and write *T* (true) or *F* (false) next to the statements.

_____ 1 The text will only describe modern types of transportation.

_____ 2 The text will mainly focus on one type of transportation.

_____ 3 The text will discuss ways people commute.

Read the article. Then answer the questions that follow.

Transportation in India

1 India has a population of 1.2 billion. However, only 6% of households own cars. How do so many people in this growing country get to their destinations each day?

2 One form of traditional Indian transportation is the water taxi. These boats carry thousands of passengers along the Ganges River every day. Another way to travel is by ox cart, traditionally used in the outskirts of cities and in the countryside of India. Some cities have banned ox carts and other slow moving vehicles on the main roads to reduce traffic congestion. Bicycles are also very popular in India, and more than 60% of households own at least one. But while such private modes of transportation are useful, India's public transportation systems are among the most heavily used in the world.

3 Fifty-three of India's cities have a population of over one million people, so the public transportation system is essential for urban life. The main forms of public transportation are small motor vehicles, buses, and railroads. Rickshaws, a type of small, bicycle-powered taxi, are common, too. Although some of these cities have bus systems, many people use smaller road vehicles, which results in some of the worst traffic problems in the world.

4 The railways are another popular form of public transportation. They were first introduced to India in 1853. In 1951, the many different systems were nationalized into one system, becoming one of the largest rail networks in the world. Now Indian trains carry over 23 million passengers daily. While Indian trains are safe and generally efficient, they often run late, but are still preferable to spending hours in traffic. However, with India's growing population, unless more public transportation is offered, it may not be possible to avoid long commutes.

PART B: ADDITIONAL SKILLS

2 Complete the table using words from the article.

Traditional transportation	(4) _____ transportation
(1) _____ carry commuters along the river.	Motor vehicles, buses, and (5) _____ are used in cities.
(2) _____ are used in the countryside but are not allowed in some cities.	(6) _____ are small, bicycle-powered vehicles.
More than 60% of households own (3) _____ .	Indian (7) _____ carry over 23 million passengers daily.

3 Check the statements that the author would agree with.

1 ☐ Traditional forms of transportation are the best ways to get around.
2 ☐ India needs more public transportation options.
3 ☐ Taking the train is better than driving in traffic in India.
4 ☐ Big cities need many modes of public transportation.
5 ☐ More people in India should buy cars.

Prism Reading 2 © Cambridge University Press 2018 **Photocopiable**

Name: _____ Date: _____

PART A: KEY VOCABULARY

1 Match the questions and answers.

1 Do you take **public transportation**? _____
2 Is your **destination** downtown? _____
3 Is an **emergency** causing this slow traffic? _____
4 Do you need more **fuel** for the car? _____
5 Does your city have lanes for **cycling**? _____
6 Do you work in **engineering**? _____

a No, bikes have to ride in the street with cars.
b Yes, I have to get some gas soon.
c Yes, I ride the bus to work.
d No, it's just normal rush hour delays.
e Yes, I design bridges.
f No, I'm traveling outside the city today.

2 Complete the paragraph with the correct form of the words in the box.

commuter congestion connect government outskirts practical rail vehicle

The city council is meeting to discuss traffic (1) _____ , especially during rush hour. Cars and other (2) _____ move very slowly at this time, and reports of road rage and accidents are increasing. One solution is to expand the (3) _____ system so that it reaches more areas outside the city. By extending train service to the surrounding areas and city (4) _____ , we can decrease the number of people on the roads by increasing the number of (5) _____ on the train. The purpose of today's meeting is to determine if this is a (6) _____ solution, considering the city's financial budget. We will be reviewing the costs involved in order to (7) _____ the outer areas of the city to the downtown. The city (8) _____ will make its decision in November.

PART B: LANGUAGE DEVELOPMENT

3 TRANSPORTATION COLLOCATIONS Match the words to make collocations about transportation.

1 traffic _____   a transportation
2 bike _____   b congestion
3 car _____   c hour
4 parking _____   d lane
5 public _____   e rage
6 road _____   f restrictions
7 rush _____   g pool

4 Complete the sentences with collocations from Exercise 3. You will not use all of the collocations.

1 The angry man almost hit me with his car in a moment of _____ .
2 I use the _____ that runs along the river when I cycle to work.
3 The _____ here is very unreliable. The trains and buses are always late.
4 There are _____ between 8am and 6pm, so do not leave your car on the street during the day.
5 The new rail system will carry 310,000 passengers daily, decreasing _____ on the road and air pollution caused by cars.

5 SYNONYMS FOR VERBS Replace the words in bold with academic synonyms in the box. You will not use all the synonyms.

attempt	consider	convince	prevent	produce	reduce	require	waste

1 I don't think you can **get** people to travel by bus if they want to drive. _____
2 Cameras will not **stop** further accidents. We need to lower speed limits. _____
3 The government must **think about** transportation options for areas outside the city center. _____
4 We do not **need** any more investment in public transportation. _____
5 It would be difficult to **try** to force people to take trains instead of cars to work. _____

Prism Reading 2 © Cambridge University Press 2018 **Photocopiable**

Name: _____   Date: _____

Read the article. Then answer the questions that follow.

The Morris Dance: An English Tradition

1   From the samba in Brazil to the halay in Turkey, traditional dances are part of the culture and history of many countries. One such dance in England is the morris dance. Morris dancing, also known simply as "morris," is a type of English folk dance traditionally associated with the month of May and the spring season. It is performed outdoors, usually by trained groups of women or men. However, the exact origins and history of the dance are unclear. Although some people think it can be traced to the 14th century, others point to its appearance in Shakespeare's plays in the 17th century. Finally, it is others' belief that the name comes from the Moors of North Africa.

2   No matter its origin, morris dancing is very lively. The dancers often have bells on their knees that ring loudly as they dance. The dancers are usually arranged either in two lines or in a circle facing each other. They wear different clothes, depending on which part of England they are from. Whatever their particular costume, male morris dancers usually wear white shirts with colored bands around their chests. They often wave white handkerchiefs or carry short sticks that they bang together as they dance.

3   Morris dances have a long tradition, but the dance also changes with the times. Some morris groups can trace their roots back over 150 years. More recently, morris groups have attempted new dances based on contemporary themes. In April 2012, a Wiltshire morris dance group created a series of dances that mimic the world's heaviest flying bird, the Great Bustard. This bird was hunted to extinction in the United Kingdom in 1832, but was reintroduced to Wiltshire, England in 2004. This new dance series was invented to raise British awareness of the Bustard.

PART A: KEY SKILLS

1   ANNOTATING   Follow the directions to annotate the reading.

1   Underline the topic sentence in each paragraph.

2   Circle the month the morris dance is associated with.

3   Number the three different beliefs of the dance's origins.

4   Box another word for *special clothes* in Paragraph 2.

5   Put two lines under a detail that supports the idea that the morris dance is very lively.

6   Box a synonym for *create* in Paragraph 3.

PART B: ADDITIONAL SKILLS

2   Choose the correct answers to complete the sentences.

1   The samba is a _____ .
   a Brazilian dance   b Turkish dance

2   The author wrote the article in order to _____ .
   a explain how the dance connects to culture.
   b explain how to perform the morris dance

3   Another word for *origin* is _____ .
   a beginning   b place

4   The history of the morris dance has _____ .
   a one story   b different stories

5   The information about the Wiltshire morris dance group supports the idea that _____ .
   a the morris dance is an ancient tradition
   b the morris dance shows modern ideas

Name: _____ Date: _____

PART A: KEY VOCABULARY

1 Choose the correct words that can replace the words or phrases in bold in the sentences.

1 At a job interview, **how you look** is very important.
   a your relationship   b your appearance

2 When I **meet** someone in the street, I usually smile and shake hands.
   a greet   b exchange

3 My husband and I **give each other** gifts on our wedding anniversary.
   a expect   b exchange

4 My favorite picture is a photo from Thanksgiving with all my **family members**.
   a relatives   b couples

5 There was a wonderful **party** after the wedding, and people danced late into the night.
   a reception   b ceremony

6 It's my **thought** that everyone should read the news and be aware of what's happening in the world.
   a relationship   b belief

7 A common **topic** in the news is climate change and its effect on the environment.
   a culture   b theme

8 I **think** that traditional dances will continue to be an important part of our culture.
   a appear   b expect

2 Complete the paragraphs with the correct form of the words in the box.

ceremony couple culture engaged formal relationship

We use different words to discuss our (1) _____ with people. For example, most languages have words for family members and relatives. In English, there are different terms to talk about a man and a woman as a(n) (2) _____ . In the beginning, we use the words *boyfriend* and *girlfriend*. Then when two people get (3) _____ , we call the man *fiancé* and the woman *fiancée* until they get married.

The wedding is considered a very special occasion. Many people invite their closest friends and family to the wedding (4) _____ . Although different (5) _____ around the world have different wedding traditions, in most countries the bride and groom dress in (6) _____ clothes as a way to show respect for such an important event.

Prism Reading 2 © Cambridge University Press 2018 **Photocopiable**

PART B: LANGUAGE DEVELOPMENT

3 AVOIDING GENERALIZATIONS   Read the generalizations. Use the words in parentheses to make the sentences more accurate.

1   Everyone in the United States loves football. (many people)

_____

2   The Japanese culture is quite formal. (can)

_____

3   Couples do not have a wedding celebration with friends or relatives. (sometimes)

_____

4   Couples expect you to fly to a vacation destination for their wedding. (occasionally)

_____

5   Americans always dress informally. (tend)

_____

6   Couples have receptions after their wedding ceremonies. (usually)

_____

7   People give speeches and congratulate newlyweds at the reception. (normally)

_____

8   When you visit someone's house for the first time, you are expected to bring a gift. (frequently)

_____

9   In India, people think it is impolite to say "no." (many)

_____

10   German speakers are always more direct than English speakers. (tend)

_____

4 SYNONYMS TO AVOID REPETITION   Choose the correct synonyms from the box to replace the words in bold. You will not use all the words.

brief   certain   common   important   obvious   separate   serious

1   It is **usual** for a newly married couple to go on a honeymoon. _____

2   It was not **clear** how long the ceremony would last, but we knew it would not be short.

   _____

3   We had a **short** stop in Dallas before flying to Mexico City. _____

4   People in **powerful** government positions can have a lot of influence on laws. _____

5   In **some** countries, people often get married when they are over thirty. _____

Name: _____ Date: _____

Read the article. Then answer the questions that follow.

Training the Body to Race

1 The best of the world's road cyclists ride in races which take them over 2,100 miles (3,500 kilometers) at an average speed of 28 miles per hour (45 kilometers per hour) on flat roads. How is this amazing physical achievement possible?

2 Teams who compete in the world's toughest road cycle races, like the Tour de France, credit their success to training. The riders set goals for each day's training. They also recognize the need to take regular breaks. This means that even though cyclists in training average about 770 miles (1,240 kilometers) a week, they do not train so hard that they get injured before their race.

3 Cyclists are more in shape than normal people. The best riders get twice as much oxygen from each breath as an average healthy person, so they are able to generate twice as much energy. Due to the riders' intense physical exercise, their hearts also pump blood to their muscles much faster than those of most people.

4 Naturally, because cyclists are so active, they need to eat a lot of calories. They pay attention to the nutritional value of their calories. Cyclists burn fat by not eating too many carbohydrates. However, in a race they need more calories for energy. During the Tour de France, a cyclist can consume up to 8,000 calories per day. In comparison, the average person's recommended daily amount is just 2,000 calories.

5 This kind of physical training and focus is essential in order to win a race, especially a long distance race such as the Tour de France, which takes 23 days, including only two days of rest. As a result cyclists must take their preparation seriously. Even the smallest aspect of a rider's performance could make the difference between winning and losing.

PART A: KEY SKILLS

1 MAKING INFERENCES Read the sentences. Check the boxes next to the statements that the author would agree with.

1 ☐ Long-distance cyclists are in better health than the average person.
2 ☐ Cyclists who race in the Tour de France are putting their bodies in serious danger.
3 ☐ The average person is overweight.
4 ☐ Competing in the Tour de France is something most people can do.
5 ☐ Diet is an important part of being a serious cyclist.

PART B: ADDITIONAL SKILLS

2 Complete the sentences with details from the article.

1 Most serious cyclists train by riding _____ miles a week.
2 In comparison to the average healthy person, a cyclist takes in more _____ to produce more energy.
3 On flat roads, the average cyclist in a long-distance race travels _____ miles per hour.
4 Cyclists pump more _____ to their muscles.
5 A cyclist doesn't eat too many carbohydrates and, as a result, he or she reduces _____ .

UNIT 5 LANGUAGE QUIZ

Name: _____ Date: _____

PART A: KEY VOCABULARY

1 Complete the paragraph with the correct form of the words in the box.

| active   balanced diet   campaign   junk food   moderate   obesity   recognize   self-esteem |

Educational programs in schools and advertising (1) _____ on the Internet and TV have been successful. The message is clear. Exercising and being more (2) _____ during the day makes people feel better. It can even improve people's moods and (3) _____ . In fact, research shows that even (4) _____ exercise, like going for a ten-minute walk, can make a difference in how we feel. This habit, combined with a(n) (5) _____ with lots of fruits and vegetables, leads to healthier lifestyles. However, although the message is out, three out of four men in the United States are overweight or suffer from (6) _____ . In my opinion, this is partly because healthy foods are often expensive, whereas fast food and (7) _____ are usually cheaper. We must (8) _____ that we have to make healthy foods available to everyone. We have to change both our exercise and eating habits if we want to be healthy.

2 Choose the correct words from the box to complete the sentences.

| calorie   nutritional   portion   reduce   serious |

1 If you look at the _____ value that is posted on food labels, you might be surprised.
2 Many foods have labels that say they are low in _____ , so people think the food is better for them.
3 There can be _____ effects to overeating. Weight gain leads to physical problems and disease.
4 If you want to lose weight, you have to _____ the number of calories you eat.
5 You should always look at the _____ on food labels. For example, pasta labels often show a serving size of half a cup, but most people eat at least a full cup.

PART B: LANGUAGE DEVELOPMENT

3 VERB AND NOUN FORMS   Cross out one mistake in a verb or noun form in each sentence, and write the correct form.

1 We must recognition the seriousness of the disease so we can better solve the problem of obesity. _____
2 We need to do more than reduction our calories to be healthy. _____
3 It is the responsibility of parents to encouragement their children to eat healthy foods. _____
4 If we promotion healthy bodies on TV, people will feel better about themselves. _____
5 Another thing we can change is how people look in advertise. _____

4 HEALTH AND FITNESS COLLOCATIONS   Match the sentence halves.

1 Reductions in heart _____   a activity includes walking.
2 People should pay attention to the nutritional _____   b disease are an effect of healthier eating.
3 Around the world, life _____   c exercise sleep better.
4 Physical _____   d value of the foods they buy.
5 People who get regular _____   e expectancy is increasing.

Read the essay. Then answer the questions that follow.

How Are Robots Like Us?

1 Robots are widely used today in factories, in space, and deep under water for jobs that are too dirty, boring, or dangerous for humans to do. Robots are also increasingly common in the home. Robot vacuum cleaners, lawnmowers, and other such devices have become very popular in some countries. While these robots for the home are helpful, they are nothing compared with the human-like robot ASIMO.

2 ASIMO, which has been in development by Honda Motor Company since 1986, is one of the most advanced robots in the world. Honda wanted to build a robot that could move like a human with abilities to help out in the home, play sports, and even dance. Over the years there were some problems developing a robot with these advanced movements. However, researchers soon had a robot that could walk on uneven surfaces and climb stairs. They continued to improve the model, and now ASIMO can even move out of the way of objects in its path.

3 The robot is also designed to be people-friendly. ASIMO can push a cart, and open and close doors. It can also shake hands. Standing 5 feet 2 inches (158 centimeters) tall, ASIMO looks like a child wearing a spacesuit. Like a child, it can look into the faces of adults who are sitting down. Using a camera, it can recognize some faces. With these advancements, Honda thinks ASIMO will definitely be helpful, especially for elderly people at home or those who can't walk on their own or who have other disabilities.

4 Researchers are now working on robots that can learn about the world around them and respond to human touch and voice. One concern with these advanced robots is that they will take the jobs people need. However, the main advantage of these robots is that they can help people. They can complete work that could be harmful to humans, assist people in need, and do some of the tasks humans do not want to do.

PART A: KEY READING SKILLS

1 SCANNING FOR INFORMATION   Read the questions. Scan the text for the underlined words, and answer the questions.

Question	Answer
1 What are two examples of <u>robots</u> commonly used <u>in the home</u>?	
2 What three <u>movements</u> did the researchers at <u>Honda</u> want <u>ASIMO</u> to do?	
3 What does <u>ASIMO</u> use to <u>recognize faces</u>?	
4 How <u>tall</u> is <u>ASIMO</u>?	
5 What is the <u>main advantage</u> of advanced <u>robots</u>?	

PART B: ADDITIONAL SKILLS

2 Write *T* (true) or *F* (false) next to the statements. Correct the false statements.

_____   1 Researchers are improving robots so the robots can learn about the world and drive cars.

_____

_____   2 The author thinks ASIMO is similar to other robots people commonly use in the home.

_____

_____   3 ASIMO can open doors for people.

_____

_____   4 Researchers at Honda Motor Company have been developing ASIMO since 1986.

_____

_____   5 People are worried that advanced robots will take their jobs.

_____

UNIT 6 LANGUAGE QUIZ

Name: _____   Date: _____

PART A: KEY VOCABULARY

1 Read the sentences. Complete the sentences with synonyms from the box for the words in parentheses.

artificial   essential   harmful   movement   pattern   power   prevent   unlimited

1 Some chemicals for cleaning are _____ (dangerous) for humans to breathe.

2 If you have the Internet, your access to knowledge is _____ (without end).

3 A runner's _____ (actions), such as taking small steps, are very important to winning a race.

4 Some of the world's _____ (energy) comes from burning coal and other fossil fuels.

5 If we want to _____ (stop) people from speeding, we should put cameras on all major roads.

6 There are many _____ (unnatural) flavors and chemicals in foods that are added to change their color or taste.

7 If you want to be healthy, it is _____ (necessary) to eat well and exercise.

8 I use a(n) _____ (repeating set) of letters and numbers so I can more easily remember my password.

2 Match the questions to the answers.

1 Is this your **personal** car? _____   a Yes, I need to find a ride.

2 Is the robot **helpful**? _____   b Yes, and it can pour a cup of coffee.

3 Can I use an **electronic** signature? _____   c Yes, think of a globe or a cube.

4 Can you **illustrate** the meaning of *exoskeleton*? _____   d Sure, I'll give you an example.

5 Can the robot pick up **objects**? _____   e Yes, it cleans the house.

6 Did your car **break down**? _____   f No, it belongs to my company.

7 Can you give an example of a **three-dimensional** object? _____   g No, we ask people to use a real pen.

PART B: LANGUAGE DEVELOPMENT

3 MAKING PREDICTIONS WITH MODALS AND ADVERBS OF CERTAINTY Complete the sentences about the future using modal and adverb phrases with the meaning in parentheses.

1 I _____ get the job because I couldn't answer all the questions on the interview, but I'll know for certain next week. (80% no)

2 People who don't smoke _____ live longer than those who do. (90% yes)

3 The managers _____ hire new workers later in the year, but it's hard to predict. (50% yes)

4 Computers _____ be more powerful in the future. (100% yes)

5 We _____ be able to breathe in space without special equipment. (100% no)

4 PREFIXES Match the words in the left column to the words or phrases in the right column with opposite meanings.

1 prevent _____   a make smaller

2 unsafe _____   b make bigger

3 disorganized _____   c not dangerous

4 enlarge _____   d make happen

5 decrease _____   e neat

Name: _____ Date: _____

Read the article. Then answer the questions that follow.

Blue Jeans: An American Tradition

1 Many inventions have shaped American culture. One was created many years ago but is still popular today: Levi's jeans. In my opinion, this invention is a very American story, involving an immigrant and his success.

2 Levi Strauss was born in 1829 in Bavaria, which is part of Germany today. Like many immigrants, he moved to America and settled in New York. In 1853, he moved from New York to San Francisco, where people were mining for gold. However, unlike many other hopeful travelers, Strauss didn't go to California to mine for gold. He saw a different opportunity. He became a supplier of clothes, boots, and other goods to small stores that sold these products to miners. This is how people become successful. They see a need and create a business. But this is not how Strauss made most of his money. It was through his work with Jacob Davis.

3 Davis made clothes for the many people in California who were doing hard labor, like gold mining. They needed pants that would last, so Davis used material from Strauss and added metal rivets to the pockets to prevent tearing. Davis asked Strauss to invest in the pants and Strauss saw another opportunity. Soon they were in business together. In 1873, blue jeans were for sale. As a result of the new design, demand for the product increased. Strauss opened a factory in San Francisco to manufacture the jeans and hired hundreds of workers. When he died in 1902, the company kept going.

4 By the 1920s, the miners had left California but other workers were buying Levi's. It became one of the leading brands in men's work clothing. In the 1950s, after movie stars Marlon Brando and James Dean were seen wearing them, jeans became a common item of clothing for all Americans. Today Levi's jeans are still one of the most popular products of American culture, and the Levi Strauss & Company is a multinational company with offices all over the world. Like many American inventions, I think blue jeans exist because of an immigrant's hard work and smart decisions.

PART A: KEY SKILLS

1 DISTINGUISHING FACT FROM OPINION   Look at the sentences from the reading. Check whether they are facts or the writer's opinion.

	Fact	Opinion
1 In 1853, Strauss moved from New York to San Francisco, where people were mining for gold.		
2 This is how people become successful. They see a need and create a business.		
3 In my opinion, this invention is a very American story, involving an immigrant and his success.		
4 Today Levi's jeans are still one of the most popular products of American culture, and the Levi Strauss & Company is a multinational company with offices all over the world.		
5 Like many American inventions, I think blue jeans exist because of an immigrant's hard work and smart decisions.		

PART B: ADDITIONAL SKILLS

2 Number the events in the correct order.

a Davis asked Strauss to invest in the pants. _____

b Blue jeans were for sale. _____

c People were mining for gold. _____

d Levi Strauss & Company is a multinational company. _____

e Levi Strauss became a supplier of clothes, boots, and other goods to small stores. _____

Name: _____ Date: _____

PART A: KEY VOCABULARY

1 Complete the sentences with the correct form of the words from the box that have the same meaning as the words or phrases in parentheses.

| brand   collection   cotton   import   multinational   season   textile |

1 What are your favorite clothing _____ (labels)?

2 What _____ (time of year) are most new fashions advertised in?

3 Do you know how many people work in the _____ (fabric) industry worldwide?

4 Did you buy clothes from any of the famous _____ (fashion house designs) this spring?

5 Many clothes are made from _____ (the soft cloth that is made from a plant) grown in China and India.

6 The United States _____ (buys from another country) many products from China, such as toys and clothes.

7 Some _____ (global) companies invest in the areas of the world where they have factories.

2 Complete the paragraph with the correct form of the words in the box.

| conditions   invest   manufacture   offshore   outsource   volume   wage |

In the United States, some people do not want to (1) _____ jobs to other countries. They want the jobs to stay at home, and yet many businesses have factories overseas. These businesses (2) _____ clothing, electronics, cars, and many other products in factories in other countries where they can pay workers less. Now, some people want to move those factories from (3) _____ locations back to the United States. However, I don't think it will work. Businesses are not going to pay the higher (4) _____ that American workers want. In addition, many of these businesses have already (5) _____ millions of dollars in their overseas production. They don't want to lose this money. I also don't think factories in the United States can match the (6) _____ that these overseas factories produce. There they employ millions of workers for long hours, while workers in the United States are used to jobs that last from 9a.m. to 5p.m. Finally, the working (7) _____ in the United States are generally much better but also more expensive than those for workers overseas. I'm afraid most of those manufacturing jobs have left the country for good.

PART B: LANGUAGE DEVELOPMENT

3 VOCABULARY FOR THE FASHION BUSINESS Match the numbered sentences to the correct lettered sentences.

1 Many name brands use famous people in their advertising, and it works. _____

2 My neighbors sell sports equipment to small stores and businesses. _____

3 Human rights groups are concerned about the working conditions in factories. _____

4 Many consumers wait until a product has been for sale for a while before buying it. _____

5 Big chain stores are major competitors in the fashion business. _____

a People buy the product so they can feel beautiful, talented, or strong, like the people they see.

b For instance, many people in manufacturing are paid low wages and work in unhealthy environments.

c They can compete with the famous designers because their clothes often look like expensive brands but cost much less.

d As suppliers, they make money from the businesses that sell their goods.

e They think they can then get the product for a cheaper price.

Name: _____ Date: _____

Read the article. Then answer the questions that follow.

Healthy Economies, Healthy Societies

1 The citizens in countries ruled by democratic governments are used to regular elections. Governments change, but often it takes time before there is an effect on a country's economic growth. However, the situation can be different in countries ruled by people who are not voted into power.

2 When a government falls suddenly, the country's economy can experience major difficulties. Interest rates often rise, natural resources may not be protected, and the economy can suffer. This loss of wealth can lead to poverty and to a recession. One reason for this is a decrease in investment from overseas. A typical pattern follows: a country's leader falls, foreign investors leave, there is a sharp decrease in the market value of the money, people lose jobs, and business sales fall.

3 Despite this situation, many investors put their money into overseas financial institutions, which can offer high returns. However, they must be aware of the risks involved. Business people may benefit from high interest rates offered by banks overseas, but this model can often not be sustained, and people can lose huge amounts of money. This trend was seen in 2013 in Cyprus when banks increased their loans for housing, but then home prices fell rapidly.

4 Investors looking for a safer long-term return can invest in the economy of a country rather than simply saving their money in banks. Such investments can create jobs, develop new businesses, restaurants, and shopping malls in a country. Outside wealth can turn a country's failing economy around.

5 If businesses invest in long-term projects such as factories, mining, and other resources needed for manufacturing, a country's economy can improve. In addition, governments have a major role in the investment of money and resources in the country. Through government spending and taxation, their countries' economies can become more stable, and their societies can benefit as people gain access to healthcare, housing, and jobs.

PART A: KEY SKILLS

1 SKIMMING Skim the text. Check the topics that the text discusses.

1 ☐ the effects on an economy when a government changes quickly
2 ☐ the rules for democratic elections
3 ☐ the risk involved with investing in overseas financial institutions
4 ☐ investment options for long-term growth
5 ☐ the government's responsibility in maintaining the economy

UNDERSTANDING LINE GRAPHS

Look at the graph about U.S Home Ownerships. Then, complete Exercises 1 and 2.

2 Choose the correct words to complete the paragraph about the graph.

This graph shows there was (1) *a slight rise / rise slightly* in U.S. home ownership until 2005. While home ownership did not (2) *fall dramatically / dramatic fall*, the percentage of homeowners from 2005 to 2015 clearly (3) *decreased / increased*. Rather than showing considerable fluctuations, the graph shows that overall there was a (4) *slight increase / slight decrease* in homeownership in the first ten years and a (5) *gradual decrease / sharp decrease* in the next ten years.

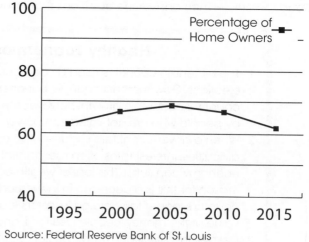

Home Ownership in the United States

Source: Federal Reserve Bank of St. Louis
(https://fred.stlouisfed.org/series/RHORUSQ156N#0)

3 Use *from, to, and, of,* or *between* to complete the paragraph about the graph.

(1) _____ 1995 to 2005, U.S. home ownership increased. (2) _____ 2005 and 2015, home ownership decreased. There was an increase (3) _____ 3% in home ownership between 1995 (4) _____ 2000. Overall, the percentage of U.S. home owners from 1995 (5) _____ 2015 decreased.

PART B: ADDITIONAL SKILLS

4 Complete the summary with the correct form of the words in the box. There is one extra word.

business   sale   economy   election   interest   investment
manufacturing   natural resource   overseas   recession   standard of living

Some countries hold regular (1) _____ and although there is a change in the government, the effects on the economy are not immediate. However, when a governments fails, a country's (2) _____ can suffer. When important (3) _____ such as coal, wood, and oil are not managed well, the economy can decline dramatically. When an economy suffers badly, the country can experience negative growth. This is known as a (4) _____ , and it usually includes the loss of jobs and can lead to poverty. This situation can happen when there is a sudden loss of (5) _____ coming from other countries. A drastic fall in the value of a country's money can lead to a decrease in (6) _____ because people can no longer afford the prices charged by stores. Some financial institutions offer high (7) _____ rates; however, investors risk losing a lot of money if the market fails. Money from investors can help foreign countries, especially when the money goes toward developing jobs and businesses in these (8) _____ countries. For instance, economies will become more stable if businesses invest in large projects such as those needed for the (9) _____ industry. The government is also important. It can direct money to the resources people need to improve their (10) _____ .

Prism Reading 2 © Cambridge University Press 2018 **Photocopiable**

UNIT 8 LANGUAGE QUIZ

Name: _____ Date: _____

PART A: KEY VOCABULARY

1 Match the answers to the questions.

1 Did your **income** increase? _____

2 Has your **standard of living** decreased? _____

3 Do you have much money in **savings**? _____

4 Is the country in a **recession**? _____

5 Do you spend a large **percentage** of your salary on rent? _____

6 Do you make a good **return** on your investments? _____

7 Do you pay a high **interest rate** on your car loan? _____

8 Do you own **stocks and shares**? _____

a No, job growth is up, and the economy is doing well.

b Not really. I get about 3% annually from them.

c Yes, I got a 5% raise last year.

d Yes, I've been putting money in the bank since I was 15.

e No, I don't invest in the stock market.

f Yes, ten years ago I could afford more things.

g Yes, the bank charges me 10%.

h Yes, 40% of my income goes to housing.

2 Write the correct form of the words in the box with the same meaning as the words or phrases in parentheses.

expenditure   factor   investment   investor   value

1 Did the _____ (worth) of your home go down in the recession?

2 Buying property is usually a good _____ (way to make money).

3 What _____ (money spent) do you have each month?

4 Do you know any _____ (people who put money into businesses) who can give me financial advice?

5 What are the main _____ (reasons) that lead to a recession?

PART B: LANGUAGE DEVELOPMENT

3 NOUNS AND ADJECTIVES FOR ECONOMICS Cross out the incorrect noun or adjective form in each sentences. Write the correct form.

1 The country has been in a poor finance state since the decline of the manufacturing industry. _____

2 We need to invest in programs that help poverty people. _____

3 This is the kind of investment our economic needs to avoid recession. _____

4 Houses have fallen in valuable over the past few years. _____

5 She could not find employed as an architect so she decided to go back to school. _____

4 NOUNS FOR ECONOMIC TRENDS Complete the paragraph with the correct form of the words in the box.

consumer   demand   market   purchase   trend

In the last few years, more and more people have been buying homes. This (1) _____ is taking place in cities and in suburbs. As the (2) _____ for homes increases, home prices go up. Overall, this is good for the housing (3) _____ , which has had problems. In addition to home (4) _____ , research shows that people are making other big expenditures. As a result, the economy is improving as (5) _____ spend money.

Prism Reading 2 © Cambridge University Press 2018 **Photocopiable**

UNIT QUIZZES ANSWER KEY

UNIT 1 READING QUIZ

PART A: KEY SKILLS

1 c

2 a 2 b 1 c 3

Part B: Additional Skills

3 1 T

2 F; The Portuguese man-of-war floats in warm waters. It cannot swim.

3 F; The tentacles can grow up to 165 feet (50 meters) long.

4 F; The sting is fatal for most fish, but it isn't usually fatal for humans.

5 T

6 T

UNIT 1 LANGUAGE QUIZ

PART A: KEY VOCABULARY

1 1 b 2 a 3 b 4 a 5 b 6 b 7 b
8 a 9 a

2 1 endangered 2 survive 3 destroy 4 native
5 protect 6 cruel

PART B: LANGUAGE DEVELOPMENT

3 1 a 2 a 3 b 4 b 5 b

4 1 stronger than 2 more common than
3 more dangerous than 4 larger than
5 heavier than

UNIT 2 READING QUIZ

PART A: KEY SKILLS

1 a huge moving masses of ice

b 75%

c 25%

d The glaciers melt faster than they grow.

e Fish and other sea life depend on water temperatures, which are changing. OR Many of the world's islands are in danger of flooding.

PART B: ADDITIONAL SKILLS

2 1 melt 2 rise 3 ice 4 snow 5 growing
6 25 7 1/3 8 75 9 billion 10 19

UNIT 2 LANGUAGE QUIZ

PART A: KEY VOCABULARY

1 1 Logging 2 rainforests 3 threatened
4 global warming 5 atmosphere
6 greenhouse gases

2 1 c 2 e 3 i 4 b 5 d 6 g 7 f 8 a 9 h

PART B: LANGUAGE DEVELOPMENT

3 1 challenges 2 predict 3 annual 4 trend
5 contribute to

4 1 plants 2 environmental 3 climate
4 tropical 5 greenhouse

UNIT 3 READING QUIZ

PART A: KEY SKILLS

1 1 F 2 F 3 T

PART B: ADDITIONAL SKILLS

2 1 Water taxis 2 Ox carts 3 bicycles
4 Public 5 railroads 6 Rickshaws
7 trains/railways

3 2, 3, 4

UNIT 3 LANGUAGE QUIZ

PART A: KEY VOCABULARY

1 1 c 2 f 3 d 4 e 5 a 6 b

2 1 congestion 2 vehicles 3 rail 4 outskirts
5 commuters 6 practical 7 connect
8 government

PART B: LANGUAGE DEVELOPMENT

3 1 d 2 g 3 f 4 a 5 e 6 c 7 b

4 1 road rage 2 bike lane
3 public transportation 4 parking restrictions
5 traffic congestion

5 1 convince 2 prevent 3 consider 4 require
5 attempt

UNIT 4 READING QUIZ

PART A: KEY SKILLS

1 1 P1: From the samba in Brazil to the halay in
Turkey, traditional dances are part of the
culture and history of many countries. P2: No
matter its origin, morris dancing is very lively.
P3: Morris dances have a long tradition, but
the dance also changes with the times.

2 May

3 (1) Although some people think it can be
traced to the 14th century, (2) others point to
its appearance in plays by Shakespeare in
the 17th century. (3) Finally, it is others' belief
that the name comes from the Moors of
North Africa.

4 costume

5 The dancers often have bells on their knees
that ring loudly as they dance. / They often
wave white handkerchiefs or carry short
sticks that they bang together as they
dance.

6 invented

PART B: ADDITIONAL SKILLS

2 1 a 2 a 3 a 4 b 5 b

UNIT 4 LANGUAGE QUIZ

PART A: KEY VOCABULARY

1 1 b 2 a 3 b 4 a 5 a 6 b 7 b 8 b

2 1 relationships 2 couple 3 engaged
4 ceremony 5 cultures 6 formal

PART B: LANGUAGE DEVELOPMENT

3 1 Many people in the United States love
football.

2 The Japanese culture can be quite formal.

3 Couples sometimes do not have a wedding
celebration with friends or relatives.

4 Couples occasionally expect you to fly to a
vacation destination for their wedding.

5 Americans tend to dress informally.

6 Couples usually have receptions after their
wedding ceremonies.

7 People normally give speeches and
congratulate newlyweds at the reception.

8 When you visit someone's house for the first
time, you are frequently expected to bring
a gift.

9 In India, many people think it is impolite to
say "no."

10 German speakers tend to be more direct
than English speakers.

4 1 common 2 obvious 3 brief 4 important
5 certain

UNIT 5 READING QUIZ

PART A: KEY SKILLS

1 1, 5

PART B: ADDITIONAL SKILLS

2 1 28 2 oxygen 3 770 4 blood 5 fat

UNIT 5 LANGUAGE QUIZ

PART A: KEY VOCABULARY

1 1 campaigns 2 active 3 self-esteem
4 moderate 5 balanced diet 6 obesity
7 junk food 8 recognize

2 1 nutritional 2 calories 3 serious 4 reduce
5 portion

PART B: LANGUAGE DEVELOPMENT

3 1 ~~recognition~~; recognize 2 ~~reduction~~; reduce
3 ~~encouragement~~; encourage
4 ~~promotion~~; promote
5 ~~advertise~~; advertisements / advertising

4 1 e 2 d 3 b 4 a 5 c

UNIT 6 READING QUIZ

PART A: KEY SKILLS

1　1 vacuum cleaners and lawnmowers
2 help out in the home, play sports, and dance
3 a camera
4 5 feet 2 inches / 158 centimeters
5 They can help people. / They can complete work that could be harmful to humans, assist people in need, and do some of the tasks humans do not want to do.

PART B: ADDITIONAL SKILLS

2　1 F; Researchers are improving robots so robots can learn about the world and respond to human voice and touch.
2 F; While these robots for the home are helpful, they are nothing compared with the human-like robot ASIMO.
3 T
4 T
5 T

UNIT 6 LANGUAGE QUIZ

PART A: KEY VOCABULARY

1　1 harmful　2 unlimited　3 movements
4 power　5 prevent　6 artificial　7 essential
8 pattern

2　1 a　2 e　3 g　4 d　5 b　6 f　7 c

PART B: LANGUAGE DEVELOPMENT

3　1 probably won't　2 will probably
3 could possibly　4 will definitely
5 definitely won't

4　1 c　2 d　3 e　4 a　5 b

UNIT 7 READING QUIZ

PART A: KEY SKILLS

1　1 Fact　2 Opinion　3 Opinion　4 Fact
5 Opinion

PART B: ADDITIONAL SKILLS

2　a 3　b 4　c 1　d 5　e 2

UNIT 7 LANGUAGE QUIZ

PART A: KEY VOCABULARY

1　1 brands　2 season　3 textile　4 collections
5 cotton　6 imports　7 multinational

2　1 outsource　2 manufacture　3 offshore
4 wages　5 invested　6 volume　7 conditions

PART B: LANGUAGE DEVELOPMENT

3　1 d　2 b　3 e　4 c　5 a

UNIT 8 READING QUIZ

PART A: KEY SKILLS

1　1, 3, 4, 5

2　1 a slight rise　2 fall dramatically
3 decrease　4 slight increase
5 gradual decrease

3　1 From　2 Between　3 of　4 and　5 to

PART B: ADDITIONAL SKILLS

4　1 elections　2 economy　3 natural resources
4 recession　5 investments　6 sales
7 interest　8 overseas　9 manufacturing
10 standard of living

UNIT 8 LANGUAGE QUIZ

PART A: KEY VOCABULARY

1　1 c　2 f　3 a　4 h　5 d　6 b　7 g　8 e

2　1 value　2 investment　3 expenditures
4 investors　5 factors

PART B: LANGUAGE DEVELOPMENT

　1 ~~finance~~; financial　2 ~~poverty~~; poor
3 ~~economic~~; economy　4 ~~valuable~~; value
5 ~~employed~~; employment

　1 trend　2 demand　3 market　4 purchases
5 consumers

CREDITS

The authors and publishers acknowledge the following sources of copyright material and are grateful for the permissions granted. While every effort has been made, it has not always been possible to identify the sources of all the material used, or to trace all copyright holders. If any omissions are brought to our notice, we will be happy to include the appropriate acknowledgements on reprinting and in the next update to the digital edition, as applicable.

Photo credits
p. 41 (photo 1): Dinodia Photo/Passage/Getty Images; p. 41 (photo 2): Meinzahn/iStock Editorial/Getty Images Plus/Getty Images.

Front cover photographs sourced from Getty Images: Letizia Le Fur/ONOKY; Sascha Kilmer/Moment

Corpus
Development of this publication has made use of the Cambridge English Corpus (CEC). The CEC is a multi-billion word computer database of contemporary spoken and written English. It includes British English, American English, and other varieties of English. It also includes the Cambridge Learner Corpus, developed in collaboration with the University of Cambridge ESOL Examinations. Cambridge University Press has built up the CEC to provide evidence about language use that helps to produce better language teaching materials

Cambridge Dictionaries
Cambridge dictionaries are the world's most widely used dictionaries for learners of English. The dictionaries are available in print and online at dictionary.cambridge.org. Copyright © Cambridge University Press, reproduced with permission.

Typeset by QBS